SHINE

make them wonder what you've got

SHINE

make them wonder what you've got

WHITAKER
HOUSE

SHINE: MAKE THEM WONDER WHAT YOU'VE GOT

ISBN: 0-88368-772-0
Printed in the United States of America
© 2002 by Newsboys

Newsboys
712 Evans Street
Franklin, TN 37064
www.newsboys.com
e-mail: mail@fcmgt.com

Whitaker House
30 Hunt Valley Circle
New Kensington, PA 15068
Visit our web site at: www.whitakerhouse.com

Library of Congress Cataloging-in-Publication Data (PENDING)

1 2 3 4 5 6 7 8 9 10 11 12 13 /09 08 07 06 05 04 03 02

Contents

Dedication

To Summer, Breeon, Heather, Erica,
Jenny, Sharon, and Simone.
Truly you shine above rubies.

Acknowledgments

Without the following, this is all pulp, binding, and ink:

Pastors Ray and Elizabeth McCollum

Pastors Bill and Rosalie Furler

Pastors Mr. and Mrs. C.

The Rev. Mylon and Christy Lefevre

Pastor Dale Evrist

Father Phillip Breen

Pastors John and Sandy Frankenstein

Pastor Ray—your teaching is a great blessing to us. Thanks
for your words in this book.

Here's to iron that sharpens iron—Wes, Steve, Anthony,
and Steve T.

To Mums and Dads, brothers and sisters, we love you heaps.

To our friends and supporters—lots of love.

To the many authors mentioned in this book who have
lovingly planted before us so that we have been blessed to
find flowers along this narrow path.

To Jim and James and all the crew at Whitaker House.

And finally Lois, for your bravery in taking on the awful
task of putting to paper the scratchings and ramblings of
five brothers from different nations and mothers.

Preface

Over twenty years of pastoral ministry in Nashville, Tennessee, have given me wonderful opportunities to minister to many of the folks who are involved in "CCM," the Contemporary Christian Music industry. But back in 1997, a unique thing happened. I received a call from Wes Campbell, a faithful member of our church and leader of the management team that had brought the Newsboys to America. Wes presented us with a framed gold record commemorating the sale of over 500,000 copies of the Newsboys' album, *Take Me to Your Leader*. Wes told me it was because the Newsboys had gotten some of their ideas for songs from my preaching tapes and wanted to show their appreciation. At the time, I did not know any of the band members personally, but I remember how kind it was for them to do this for us.

That was just the beginning. Since then, and especially over the past two years, it's been my privilege to have an increasing amount of pastoral input into the Newsboys and their tremendous support team and staff. Right after the tragedy of "9-11," I even went out on the road with the band for five days of their "Festival Con Dios" tour. (You really get to know people when you live on a bus with them for a few days.) We've also had many rich times of Bible study together. My wife, Elizabeth, and I have gotten to know the Newsboys' families, as well. We spent all day with the group and their families last Thanksgiving. We've had lunches and breakfasts together. And after all this, I can tell you truthfully that these are some of the finest folks you'll ever meet anywhere.

I love the Newsboys. But I don't love them primarily because of their talent and gifting, even though that's tremendous. I love these guys because they are for real. They love the Lord, and they want to "shine" for Him. I've never heard them say a bad word, an off-color joke, or an unkind thing about anyone. The tour bus was equipped with satellite TV that picked up every channel the world has to offer. The first day I noticed one of the Boys was deleting all the "adult" and "movie" channels so they were blacked out of the system. There was no fanfare involved, no "holiness" speeches. It was a simple decision to block out images none of us needed to see, even in passing. That impressed me. (They did watch unending coverage of international cross-country motorcycle racing, however— not my favorite!)

Some of what you'll read here is cutting-edge insight into what it's going to take to change our culture and our world. I think you'll be impressed with how this band grasps the importance of personal discipleship and commitment to the local church.

(1) They understand that *individual* destiny can never be discovered apart from *corporate* destiny. Who we're with determines where we're going; therefore, identification with a local church is not an option. This membership is not nominal (in name only), but vital and indispensable.

(2) They understand that moral accountability insures the development of personal character. Each band member has committed to be accountable to a pastor or pastoral team and is willing to be corrected, disciplined, and held accountable for his personal life and behavior.

(3) They understand that concerts and "platform ministry" do not really permanently change lives. They know that there is no substitute for personal discipleship and follow-up and that Christian lives not grounded in foundational biblical principles won't work.

(4) They understand that the Christian life is a progressive work of sanctification and that the process is never completed this side of eternity.

(5) Finally, they understand that although the church has not been "shining" as it should, the church is still Christ's body, the foremost expression of the kingdom of God on earth and the visible "family of God." *Shine:*

Make Them Wonder What You've Got points out some of the weaknesses and shortcomings of the church in America. But this band is not standing on the outside, criticizing and judging the church. The Newsboys are "in" the church and committed to its health and well-being. *Shine* simply gives us a good look at how we can become the "salt" and "light" Jesus designed us to be.

Enjoy *Shine.* It's coming from the heart.

Pastor Ray McCollum
Bethel World Outreach Center/
Morning Star International
Nashville, Tennessee

Let your light shine before men, that they may see your good deeds and praise your Father in heaven.

—Matthew 5:16

Prelude:
An Awakening

I believed Christ was the way, but yet I was lost. I believed He was the truth, but at the same time, I was deceived. I believed He was the life, but I knew not the Life. Then, by way of mercy, trial, tragedy, and grace, there was a sifting like that of wheat, and for the first time, I started again on this journey knowing that Christ must increase, and I must disappear.   —Peter Furler

I think in the last couple of years there's been an awakening in the band to what really matters....I feel like I've become a new person, an absolutely new human being.   —Phil Joel

The events of the last year and a half or two years have really shown me that it's one thing to have your ministry and the work that you are doing. For us, it's being the Newsboys and doing our thing there. But we really got a big wake-up call a little over a year ago....

—Jody Davis

I didn't learn what grace really meant until about two years ago, and it has changed my life dramatically. I think it scares a lot of people around me because, if anything, I may present myself as what a lot of people think of as less of a Christian, when really, I'm being more honest and transparent.   —Jeff Frankenstein

I believe that God is really doing something in the spiritual realm with this band, more so than He ever has done before....I've been a Christian for a long time, probably twenty years now, and you have your times of your mountaintop experiences and then you have your other times that aren't quite so high. But I really feel that God is preparing me for something incredible, something exciting, and I think the rest of the band is feeling the same.

—Duncan Phillips

Like a song written in private, then played over a public address system, this book carries personal thoughts, secret hopes, maybe even a little wishful thinking, and sends them blaring out for everyone to hear. Or as Frederick Buechner put it, "Think of these pages as graffiti maybe, and where I have scratched up in a public place my longings and loves, my grievances and indecencies, be reminded in private of your own. In that way, at least, we can hold a kind of converse."

Many a conversation has been had among the members of the band over the years, from pubs in London, to a Greek restaurant in Detroit (lamb chops—well done, thanks), to the dirt bike trails of Baja, Mexico. These were not discussions (I guess) like those of the intelligencia or even the "super-spiritual," but instead were maybe like those of nomads or "ragamuffins" finding land with a buried treasure and dealing together with the process of selling everything they had to buy that land.

Having been with the band since its beginnings, sleeping in an old Dodge van; freezing in a harsh New York winter; sweating buckets in a Death Valley, California, summer; playing shows until my fingers bled a little bit; meeting my beautiful wife in Atlanta, Georgia; seeing the end of the days (I hope) of asking rowdy punters to step outside to deal with it Aussie style; standing in a foot of snow in Louisville, Kentucky, numb at the funeral of our friend and former bass player, K.M.—God's grace is sufficient; celebrating my tenth wedding anniversary when, suddenly, in what seemed like the twinkling of an eye, we were all standing in the foyer of Vanderbilt Hospital—band, wives, suits and ties, waiting for the doctors to tell us if Jody and Erica's baby girl was going to make it through the night; and watching the grace of God restore marriages that seemed irreparable to our human understanding; I've often thought how odd it is that life's strange happenings and times of adversity, which normally might tear a group of people apart, when offered upward, can have the reverse effect.

These are thoughts written down mainly so that we, the band, don't forget them. Maybe for us they are a little gathering of what has been our daily bread on the path to the kingdom that, the closer you get to it, the more you shine.

The truth is, we're not where we need to be, but many are witnesses that we're not (by His grace) where we used to be, either. I pray for God's favor, because the Good Lord knows that's what it's going to take! Even more, I pray that His Spirit breathes upon each word, lest we be wasting His beautiful trees.

True love and peace, only through Christ,

Peter

And the end of all our exploring
will be to arrive where we started
and know it for the first time.

—T. S. Eliot

Part I

Where's the Light?

You are the light of the world. A city on a hill cannot be hidden. Neither do people light a lamp and put it under a bowl. Instead they put it on its stand, and it gives light to everyone in the house. In the same way, let your light shine before men, that they may see your good deeds and praise your Father in heaven.

—Matthew 5:14–16

Down here in the valley
Nothing's able to grow
'Cause the light's too low
Folks spend their days
Digging 'round for diamonds and gold
'Til they just get old
And they don't know anything else
They don't know they're breathing bad air
But I'm tired of living like this
And my soul cries out, "If You're there..."

Call me up to Your side
Draw me up to Your light
Let it blind me
Lord, refine me
Refine me out of my mind

"Thrive"
Thrive

> The gospel will persuade no one unless it has so convicted us that we are transformed by it.
> —Brennan Manning

 A car with a bumper sticker that reads, "Christians aren't perfect, just forgiven," speeds down the highway, cutting someone off. As the other driver scrambles for control of her car, she sees the bumper sticker and yells in frustration, "Does being forgiven give you license to run me off the road?"

 Two teenagers meet for lunch. One wears a shirt that announces, "Jesus is the reason for the season," and the other a jacket with the words, "Jesus rules." Their lunch conversation centers on the latest church gossip. A husband and wife seated nearby exchange glances. The wife says, "If that's the way they talk about each other, I certainly wouldn't want to go to *their* church."

 A busy executive spends many hours leading the men's ministry at his church and teaching a Bible study, but he never seems to have time for his family and constantly loses his temper when he is home. Each week his children sit in the back of the room where the Bible study meets, listening to him teach the Scriptures and thinking, "Hypocrite!"

 A protester explodes a bomb at an abortion clinic, killing a doctor. As the smoke clears, the news media interviews a pro-abortion leader and an attorney who say Christians are dangerous and their beliefs promote violence.

 A demonstrator stands at the fresh grave of a murdered homosexual, holding a sign that says, "He's burning in hell." Relatives and friends, who have come to mourn their loved one, stare in shock. "If that's the way God really feels," the victim's mother says, "I hate Him!"

The driver, the teenagers displaying Christian slogans, the busy executive, the protester, and the demonstrator all have something in common. They believe they're shining the light of Christ to the world.

What's the Message?

If you had encountered these people while you were unsaved, what would you have learned from them? Would you have found their words and actions attractive—or would you have been repelled by them?

Whether we're dealing with controversial issues such as abortion and homosexuality or everyday situations such as driving to work, eating out, and serving at church, what we do and how we act speak volumes to those around us.

Because we are Christians, when people hear the name of Jesus, they see a picture of us in their minds. How we live our lives sends a message to them about who Jesus is and what the Christian faith is all about.

If someone were to give a description of the Gospel just from observing your life, what do you think that person would say? What message is your life proclaiming?

> Through our lives people learn the
> message of the Gospel. If what we
> say and what we do don't match up,
> we create confusion and cause people
> to reject the message.

That very question has been burning in our hearts and minds. As the Newsboys, through our albums and tours, we have some degree of contact with hundreds of thousands of people. We're grateful when people are blessed by our music. But in learning what it really means to "seek first the kingdom of God," we have begun to ask ourselves: What about those who know us best or interact with us personally? Do our families and friends see the light of Christ in us? What do our neighbors think of the way we demonstrate our faith? Do we treat people the way

Christ would when we address a clerk at Home Depot or talk with a ticket taker at the airline when the flight is two hours late?

Some of these things might sound insignificant on the surface. Does it really matter if we snap at a waiter because he gave us the wrong change or if we make a sarcastic remark about the way someone is dressed? We may not think so, but these actions are very significant in God's eyes because we're meant to do what Christ would do in every situation we're in. Through our lives, people learn the message of the Gospel. If what we say and what we do don't match up, we create confusion and cause people to reject the message. For example—

Could a christ who impatiently snapped at a waiter—someone who is likely tired from working for hours on his feet—then turn around and say to him, "Come to me, all you who are weary and burdened, and I will give you rest"?

Could a christ who made a sarcastic remark about someone's taste in clothes be credible when he said, "A new command I give you: Love one another. As I have loved you, so you must love one another"?

Could a christ who held a sign at someone's grave, saying, "He's burning in hell," then say, "God did not send his Son into the world to condemn the world, but to save the world through him"?

There is a vital connection between what we say and what we do. Our actions either give credibility to our words—or undermine their validity. We must earn the right to be listened to.

The Scripture says, "The Word became flesh and made his dwelling among us." When Jesus came to earth, He was the personification of the Word. It wasn't just His words, but His very life, that was the message of the Good News.

When we receive Christ into our lives, He no longer just makes His dwelling *among* us, as He did when He was living on earth, but He dwells *within* us. When we allow Him to live His life through us, our lives become the Word personified, just as His life was. It is not just our words that speak the Good News. We are living and walking pictures of Christ.

The one thing that is central to the message of the Gospel is the one thing that we seem to forget so easily—

Our *lives* are the message.

The Gospel is about transformation—the transformation of our lives by the life of Christ within us. We have to ask ourselves: Do our lives reflect the grace, truth, and love we have received through Christ? Or do they reveal that we haven't allowed the Spirit of Christ to transform us into His image so that only He shines through?

The Light of the World

Jesus described Himself as "the light of the world," but He also described His followers in the same way, saying, "You are the light of the world." When He returned to the Father, He placed the world in the care of believers, telling us that we are now to be its light, just as He was the light while He lived on earth.

At the same time, He gave us vital insight about how to be the light when He added, "*Let* your light shine." Jesus' statement shows that we need to *enable* the light to shine. It's not something that happens automatically.

It is the nature of light to illuminate. However, if something is blocking the source of that light, a shadow is created—and the full strength of the light can't be seen. If the world is having difficulty seeing the light clearly in us, then there are things in our lives that are blocking it—obstacles that are casting shadows and obscuring the power of the message.

Each one of us must discover what those obstacles are in his or her own life. However, as we have observed contemporary Christianity—and our own lives—we have noticed several obstacles many of us have in common that prevent a clear illumination of Christ to our culture. Understanding how to deal with these "shadow-casters" will go a long way in enabling us to be the light of the world.

Shadow-Casters

The Pace of Our Lives

The first obstacle may sound simple, but it has massive ramifications in our lives. It has to do with our contemporary lifestyles. Like everyone else in our culture, we are busy and exhausted. From corporate executives to grade school children, our lives are scheduled from morning to night. We're trying to keep up with work, school, family, church, and other activities. We have cell phones pressed to both ears, pagers beeping, E-mail and faxes coming in, so that we're simply overloaded with information and the demands of always being "on call."

Daily life for most families means running to sports or music practices, juggling jobs and school and friends, doing homework, making meals, taking care of the house and garden—the list goes on. Kids get tired and stressed, and parents become anxious and exhausted. Most families don't even eat meals together or spend time enjoying each other's company. They have become "strangers living under one roof"—preventing them from shining the light of Christ to one other and often setting themselves up for emotional problems, family turmoil, and even substance abuse as they try to cope alone with the pressures of life.

Then there are church activities. We can sometimes get so involved in meetings and outreaches that we have

no time left for God Himself—let alone our families and friends.

Of course, many of the activities we're involved in aren't bad in themselves. But it is possible to be involved in good things for God and still miss out on what's most important. The problem is that we're neglecting the area of our lives that needs attention if we're going to shine: our spirits. We may be active and accomplishing many things, but we can't live at this pace of life for very long and have time to reflect on our priorities and nurture our inner

> Our problem is that we're neglecting
> the area of our lives that needs
> attention if we're going to shine:
> our spirits.

lives. Our spirits are starving because one of the first things that seems to get shortchanged is our relationship with our heavenly Father. Once we lose connection with the Source, our light grows increasingly weak. It is impossible to "seek first the kingdom of God" without that connection.

We also neglect our bodies and souls, not realizing that when they don't receive the care and attention they need, it can have a negative spiritual effect on us. Physical exhaustion and emotional isolation do take a spiritual toll. Our bodies need more than activity. They can't keep functioning non-stop; they need rest and renewal. Our souls need more than information and stimulus. We need to develop relationships with our families, friends, and neighbors that go deeper than surface interaction. Since our band is on the road so much of the time doing tours, spending long hours traveling, recording, and performing, we know how easy it can be to lose those spirit- and soul-sustaining connections with God and other people—and we know the detrimental effect it can have on us spiritually.

What's hard about this "pace of life" obstacle is that it affects us gradually, so we don't notice that it is happening. It's not like being suddenly plunged into darkness, as in a blackout. Instead, the light of Christ is slowly encroached upon, just like a late-afternoon shadow invades a sunny patch of lawn. Many of us are unaware of our condition until an internal or external crisis forces us to look at what's happened. That's when the realization hits that we haven't felt at peace for a long time or that something vital is missing from our lives. The numerous expectations that have been placed upon us—either by ourselves or others—are making us uneasy and restless. Anxiety is invading our thoughts. So many things are distracting and sidetracking us from what's really important that we wonder if there's any meaning left in our lives. The thought may even cross our minds, "Is God still out there somewhere, or am I alone in this?"

Frazzled and exhausted, we go around trying to be the light of the world when the light is being blocked from our own view. In addition to all this, we feel guilty because we know we aren't making a difference in pushing back

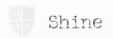

the darkness in our culture. However, we keep struggling along, trying to be a light where we can, because we remember Jesus' words—

> You are the salt of the earth. But if the salt loses its saltiness, how can it be made salty again? It is no longer good for anything, except to be thrown out and trampled by men. You are the light of the world. A city on a hill cannot be hidden. Neither do people light a lamp and put it under a bowl. Instead they put it on its stand, and it gives light to everyone in the house. In the same way, let your light shine before men, that they may see your good deeds and praise your Father in heaven.

We carry around these words like a burden on our backs. The responsibility seems too overwhelming, and despair sets in. We're tired of trying to be something we're not. Why did Jesus have to leave *us* with the job of making Him known in the world? Doesn't He know that just making it through the day is hard enough? Doesn't He know how often we mess up? Maybe we should give up trying....

Feelings of failure and despair can sometimes lead Christians to totally give up on their calling to be the light. Other believers experience the same feelings of failure, but they go around with smiles on their faces, pretending that everything is okay. Because they feel they have to have all the answers, these Christians end up wearing themselves out as they strive to keep up spiritual appearances. Rather than casting their cares on the Lord and trusting Him to live His life through them, they're continually burning their own coals, so that their spiritual lives are perpetually depleted. Other Christians react to their discouragement by slipping into a lifestyle where they hardly acknowledge God any longer and take on the attitudes and perspectives of the world—becoming barely distinguishable from the rest of society.

All these believers face a genuine dilemma because Jesus said, "If then the light within you is darkness, how great is that darkness!"

Since we are salt and light, we feel it's all up to us to change things.

"Us Versus Them"

Another obstacle that prevents the light of Christ from shining through us is a misunderstanding of what it means to proclaim the message of the Gospel to the world.

When Jesus told parables about the kingdom of God, He said we're supposed to have the same effect on society that yeast has on bread when it works its influence all the way through the dough, causing it to rise. In other words, we're to influence all aspects of society with the Gospel so that, ultimately, it can be totally transformed. He also talked about how we are to preserve the culture from corruption as salt preserves meat. For years, we have heard sermons and talks urging us to act on our responsibility to society. If Christians don't function as yeast and salt, society will continue to deteriorate. It's up to *us* to change things.

In response to this urging, many believers have tried to preserve what is good and transform what is bad in our culture. To do this, we've decided we won't let anyone silence our witness in the public arena or treat us as second-class citizens. We will demand an equal voice in policy and social matters.

Increasingly, this has become the primary focus of many Christians' outreach to the culture. Being the light of the world has come to mean announcing to the world what we believe and making sure we have a right not only to believe it, but also to say it publicly. Though there have been some setbacks, there has been significant success in achieving this goal. For the most part, we have preserved our right to express our faith and preach the Gospel.

There is certainly a need to exercise our social and political freedoms. But the difficult question then becomes, How much have we really achieved? Have we illuminated the light of Christ in society so that it is changing people's hearts and making a significant difference in their lives? Or have we traded changing hearts for merely changing laws—as good as those laws may be?

We have asserted our prerogative to be part of the culture. Yet have we made ourselves just one more special interest group striving to be heard? We must ask if we have fought for our rights to proclaim the Gospel only to become another subculture in society rather than "a holy nation, a people belonging to God, who declare the praises of Him who has called us out of darkness into His wonderful light."

Most of all, has the reason for proclaiming our faith really been motivated by a desire to be the light of the world? Or has it been the result of *fear*—fear of losing our rights, status, and influence in the world?

Will winning those things mean we've won the world for Christ?

In the larger scheme of things, have we been merely justifying our position and promoting ourselves—or have we promoted the interests of God's kingdom?

Some years ago, we recorded a song called "Not Ashamed." This song was based on a turning point in Peter's life. He had reached a place in his faith where he had settled for himself the question of, "Who is Jesus, really?" The song was meant to express, "I've truly found Christ. I believe that He is who He says He is." That's an affirmation that every Christian has to come to for himself or herself. If we believe Jesus is who He says He is, as the Scriptures attest, then we must recognize how that belief should influence every area of our lives, and we need to commit to Him and follow Him wholeheartedly. And that's what the song was about.

When "Not Ashamed" was released, it struck a chord because many Christians were uncertain about declaring what they believed. There was a hesitancy about acknowledging who Christ is. But this is no longer the case for most Christians, and the original meaning of the song has been forgotten. Slowly, over the years, the message of "not ashamed" has come to mean something entirely different for many believers.

As we have become bold in declaring our belief in God to society, we have become a generation of Christians who are no longer timid. Gone are the days when we were embarrassed to identify with the name of Jesus or when we would hide our faith for fear of being ridiculed. Although this new courage started out to be something positive, in the end, it has turned into something negative. "I'm not ashamed" has become a kind of battle cry, an anthem proclaiming: "Jesus rules, so the world can shove off!"

This "macho Christian" attitude is a misinterpretation of the Gospel because it does not reflect the nature of Christ—servanthood, compassion, and sacrifice. It is blocking the light of Christ from the world because, instead of being ambassadors of reconciliation, we have become ambassadors of Christian pride. What started out as a desire to be bold for Christ is now promoting an arrogant attitude that is creating misunderstanding, suspicion, and fear between us and the world.

An "us versus them" stance is fatal to the presentation of the Gospel because it is the place where grace dies. Our dealings with the world are no longer about reconciliation, but confrontation. It is like the parable Jesus told of the man who was forgiven a huge debt that he could never repay, but then he went out and beat up another man who owed him practically nothing. Once we've been forgiven, somehow we forget that the only difference between "us" and "them" is *grace.*

Once we've been forgiven,
we forget that the only
difference between "us" and
"them" is grace.

There's a lot of this "gung ho" Christianity in the church. Christian music festivals draw tens of thousands of people, and the Christians who gather there are certainly not ashamed. They openly display symbols of the faith. Bumper stickers, T-shirts, and jewelry all proclaim the name of Jesus. Today, it's the "cool" thing for kids to wear T-shirts with Christian messages, whereas ten years ago you were considered radical if you wore shirts like that to school. Now, everyone in every youth group does it.

Sometimes we have the idea that wearing and displaying these messages of our faith is the sum total of what it

means to be a witness, instead of recognizing that we ourselves are that witness. We're bewildered when our efforts to show the truth of the Gospel to the world seem to come back and hit us in the face. When people aren't interested in the message, we can feel increasingly isolated from the mainstream of society.

One reason for people's rejection of the message is that some of the slogans have become more offensive than thought-provoking. For example, there is a popular bumper sticker that says, "If you think you're perfect, just try walking on water." What is that really saying to people? Our Christian culture can be so perfectionist that it scares people away. When we act as if we have everything figured out, it comes off as self-righteous and judgmental. People see Christians who apparently "have it all figured out," and they think, "Well, I'm not nearly good enough for that." Or, as we mentioned before, they see the inconsistency of what we *say* we believe and what we *do*—and then write us off entirely.

Another outcome of the "not ashamed" attitude is that it has a tendency to promote selfishness. The result is that we become isolated not only from the world, but also from our brothers and sisters in the body of Christ. Christianity becomes all about "me"—my church, my bumper stickers, my T-shirts—so that we're almost in competition with other believers to see who can be the trendiest. While we think we're showing our *difference* from the world by displaying the latest Christian fad, we're actually copying the spirit of the world.

There really isn't anything wrong with most of these displays. We can use them and enjoy them. The problem comes when we allow them to become substitutes for true expressions of faith. For all the fish on our cars, hats, bags, and Bibles, have we allowed ourselves to focus on surface expressions of faith while neglecting the development of our inner character? Do we wear our Christian T-shirts declaring our faith in a loving, merciful God, but then gossip against one another or refuse to forgive each other?

> We need to be strong in our faith, but not by our own might. Sometimes we forget that we weren't born Christians.

Do we display our Ichthys-eating-Darwin stickers on our cars, but then drive like maniacs? Do we quote, "God is not willing that any should perish," but then gloat over the predicaments of unbelievers with an attitude of, "I told you so"?

The prideful "not ashamed" approach just isn't working— and it is never going to work. We need to be strong in our faith, but not by our own might. Right now, this attitude has gone over the top. It's a frenzy. A *graceless* frenzy. For the most part, we're not as concerned about reaching the unsaved for Christ as we are about proving we're better than they are. We act as if we were never in their position in the first place—or never would have gotten in their position. In other words, sometimes we forget that we weren't born Christians. Each of us had to make a choice to repent and turn our lives over to God, and that choice was made only under the umbrella of God's grace.

Therefore, we need a paradigm shift, a new way of thinking about our faith, because faith that is based on "us versus them" will not stand. It is going to get washed away because the foundation is just sand. This is one reason we're seeing massive turnover in youth groups. Kids come, and they attend for a couple of years. Then they turn eighteen, and heading to Fort Lauderdale for a good time looks like a lot more fun than being part of a group that doesn't display much grace. Maybe this is because our focus has become what we are *against* rather than what we are *for.*

Jesus said, "By this all men will know that you are my disciples, if you love one another." If people don't recognize the light of Christ in us, it could be because our lack of love, for each other as well as for the world, is blocking its radiance.

The World as We (Don't) Know It

The third obstacle is related to the second. It has to do with the increasing isolation of Christians from the rest of society. Although we are obviously meant to be "in the world but not of it," we're not meant to be so cut off from it that we can't effectively communicate the love of Christ. But this is what has happened to many believers.

There is confusion in the body of Christ over how we are to interact with the culture. The "us versus them" perspective has caused us to believe that people first have to come around to our way of thinking before we will talk to them about Christ. We don't feel we need to understand how the world thinks and feels because, we reason to ourselves, "Why should I spend my time with the world's philosophies and beliefs if they're all false, anyway?" We tell people, "Look, you need to be like us!" without taking the time to patiently and lovingly bring Christ to where *they* are. We forget that Jesus was the friend of tax collectors, prostitutes, and other "sinners" and that He brought them the Good News of the kingdom of God.

We wonder why people can't relate to what we're saying, although the Bible clearly says, "The man without the Spirit does not accept the things that come from the Spirit of God, for they are foolishness to him, and he cannot understand them, because they are spiritually discerned." The world can't understand us, and we don't feel the need to understand the world, so the chasm between us never gets bridged.

In *Learning the Language of Babylon: Changing the World by Engaging the Culture*, Terry Crist describes the bewilderment many Christians have over the state of the world we're now living in: "How did we go from being the social majority to being cultural captives in three generations?" Crist compares the situation of Christians today to the Jews in Daniel's time who were in captivity in Babylon and faced living in a culture that was the antithesis of their own beliefs. He says that if we're to be the light of the world, we have to understand the world we're living in and learn its "language." This is because the landscape of the world has changed, and we're living in a postmodern culture. Refusing to accept this reality causes us to try to be a light to the world as we *think* it should

> Our first step should be to learn the way the postmodern world thinks and lives. Otherwise, we won't be able to address the real needs of the people.

be, rather than to the world as it *actually is*. Our first step should be to learn the way the postmodern world thinks and lives. Otherwise, we won't be able to address the real needs of real people.

Pastor Dietrich Bonhoeffer, who was martyred by the Nazis in 1945, encountered a similar cultural divide to what we're experiencing today. He witnessed the loss of religious belief and church attendance among the German people. Bonhoeffer recognized that the people no longer understood the language of the church. He felt deeply that the church would have to step back and focus on prayer and righteous actions as its witness until it found a new language that could communicate spiritual truths to the contemporary mind. Developing this new language would take patience and a willingness to learn—it would require the hard work of making an effort to truly understand the minds and hearts of the people and then connecting with them.

Jesus went from the glory of heaven
to a sinful world. His love for us
caused Him to take extreme measures.
We must do the same thing, motivated
by the same love.

When we encounter the values and mind-set of contemporary society, we often respond by thinking, "I wish the world were like this, and since it isn't, I'll retreat into my safe community and have no contact with it." It is natural to want to run away from what is unpleasant to us. However, we can't be the light of the world when we have no personal contact with it and don't understand the way it thinks and feels.

One definition of postmodernism is "the fragmentation and promiscuous trivialization of values, symbols, and images." People living in a culture where what is true

and real has been trivialized will welcome an authentic manifestation of the life of Christ when it is communicated consistently and with love so that the difference is inescapable.

Increasing our interaction with a world that does not acknowledge Christ as Lord may not feel comfortable at first, but we can remember the example of Jesus. He went from the glory of heaven into a sinful and hostile world. His love for humanity caused Him to take extreme measures to win us back to God. We must do the same for the world today, motivated by the same love—while, at the same time, being careful not to become absorbed by the very world we're trying to reach.

Sometimes, in an effort to bridge the cultural gap, or because we find ourselves drawn into the mind-set of society, we think that to reach the world we have to keep up with the world's trends. Frankly, that is just rubbish. Our real need is to get back to what is true, to get back to the Gospel of the kingdom of God. Christianity has been around for two thousand years. It is never going to be trendy, because trends come and go, but the church—and the Word of God—are eternal. They have survived every trend.

Today, many of us are tempted to make the Christian faith into something that sounds appealing to people's self-interests, as if it's merely a self-help method. Yet this approach ignores the reality of our need to die to ourselves and take up our cross daily in order to follow Christ. The Gospel is the Good News, but it's not always the news we want to hear, and it's not always packaged in the way we want to view it. We need to get back to the basics of the Gospel because if we try to make it trendy, we will fail. Our efforts to do this are already failing. People need to know God's reality.

If the world can't see the light of Christ in us, it may be because we have hidden ourselves from its view entirely, or because we look so much like it. Continuing

> The Gospel is the Good News, but it's not always the news we want to hear, and it's not always packaged in the way we want to view it.

to isolate ourselves from the world or to imitate its trends will cast an even bigger shadow between Christ and our culture.

The Life Is the Light

All these obstacles are the result of a single cause: We are trying to shine by our own efforts instead of allowing Jesus to shine through us. When Jesus said, "You are the light," we hear, "*You* are the light," and we think the light has to come from us. So we try to generate the light ourselves. After a few attempts, it should become obvious that we just don't have the power. But we keep trying anyway. The Scripture says, "In him was life, and that life was the light of men." This is a massive principle to remember: The *light* comes only from the *life*—the life of Christ in us.

Let's ask ourselves, "Whose light are we trying to shine— ours or Christ's?" Without the manifestation of His life, we wouldn't even glimmer, because none of us has life in ourselves—that's a divine quality. Jesus said, "For as the Father has life in himself, so he has granted the Son to have life in himself." We *must* depend on Christ for our life.

> The light comes only from
> the life—the life of Christ
> in us.

All the obstacles that we have allowed to block the light can be used for good, if we allow them to teach us how to stop struggling in our own strength and start relying on Christ. They also can help us realize we're not all that different from the people we're supposed to be reaching out to. Those who are in the dark need the light. That is as true for us as it is for the world.

This book is called *Shine: Make Them Wonder What You've Got*. There is a reason that "Shine" comes *before*

"Make Them Wonder" in the title. It is a truth we often forget or ignore: We can't make people wonder about Christ if our light isn't first shining. We can't make them wonder what we've got if we haven't got it! So when Christ says, "Let your light shine," He is saying, in essence, "Remember who the Light is. Let Me shine through you."

Jesus said, "A city on a hill cannot be hidden." With this description, He defines us as a city whose lights can be seen even by those far away, because it is high up on a hill. We can be a light to those closest to us *and* to those who observe us from afar if we stay on that hill, because it is the city *on a hill* whose light cannot be hidden.

Too often we think the hill is a symbol of our being noticed for doing good things. This is because, a couple of verses later, we read, "Let your light shine before men, that they may see your good deeds." But the hill is *Jesus.* We're just the city. We can't do the truly good deeds if we're not relying on Him to live His life through us. When we start thinking *we're* the hill, then we are no longer resting on Him. We have slid down the hill into a valley of our own making. People can't see the light from there. Jesus said that trying to shine in our own strength is like lighting a lamp and then hiding it under a bowl. It can't do what it was intended to do.

Why aren't we the hill? It is because there is nothing about *us* that raises us higher than other people. Everything we are as the light of the world comes from our being set on the hill. King David said in one of his psalms, "Lead me to the rock that is higher than I." Christ is our Rock. If we are not abiding in Him, we're going to be on shaky ground.

> Why do you call me, "Lord, Lord," and do not do what I say? I will show you what he is like who comes to me and hears my words and puts them into practice. He is like a man building a house, who dug down deep and laid the foundation on rock. When a flood came, the torrent struck that house but could not shake it, because it was well built. But the one who hears my words and does not put them into practice is like a man who built a house on the ground without a foundation. The moment the torrent struck that house, it collapsed and its destruction was complete.

We aren't anything without Christ as our High Ground. To shine, we need to let Christ lift us out of the valley of ourselves and our own efforts and set us back on the Rock. Then His light will no longer be hidden—not to ourselves and not to the world.

"Be the Change You Want to See"

In the end, it comes down to this: The more we allow the life of Jesus to show through own lives, the more we will shine. The less we allow the life of Christ to show through us, the less we will shine. Jesus said, "The man who walks in the dark does not know where he is going. Put your trust in the light while you have it, so that you may become sons of light."

There is no better way to make a meaningful impact on the world than by becoming God's children of light—by living lives that are so free of obstructions that His light is unhindered. People today don't accept what they hear at face value. They want to know that it works. They want to *see* that it works. If not, they'll move on to something else. They're not very different from us. They have problems, needs, questions, and hopes. But they won't necessarily recognize that these things can be answered only in Christ without seeing that fact demonstrated—in *us*. We are the hope of this world, because as we reflect Christ's life, we enable them to see Him clearly.

As Christians, we're walking on "holy ground" as we live our lives before God. But holy ground is not a ground of "us versus them." Nor is it a ground where we can proudly say, "We're saved, and you're going to hell." When we are truly changed by God, suddenly we realize that all of us—the saved and the "sinners"—are equal in our need for God. We all start with the same slate. The Bible says, "There is no one righteous, not even one." God's grace— not our own—is the only thing that makes the difference.

In essence, if you want to change the world, you have to be changed first. To borrow from a famous phrase, you have to—

"Be the change you want to see."

This is because the kingdom of God does not work from the outside in but from the inside out. Jesus taught this principle in a number of ways. It is what He meant when He said we need to take the log out of our own eye before we can take the splinter out of someone else's eye. It is what He meant by "Do to others as you would have them do to you."

We will start being effective when we stop trying to change other people and instead change ourselves. To shine, you have to fill yourself with Christ. This means you first have to empty yourself, just as Jesus emptied Himself of His heavenly glory to come into the world. It's not as if we're going to rally a bunch of Christians together, get out the vote, put our man in as president, and that will solve everything. We could do all that and still not have changed anyone in the process. If we haven't seen people transformed from the inside out, we haven't really done anything that's lasting.

However, when people see us truly change, when they see our integrity, when they see the way we live our lives and the way we treat our families, our neighbors, and our enemies—that will be the ultimate witness.

This book is about that change. It is about the life and teachings of Jesus that show us how to "be the change we want to see." Many of the principles are very basic, but they bring about *monumental* transformation when they're grasped and put into practice. As you begin to apply them, all of a sudden, even before you realize it, the light will start to shine, and people will become attracted to the life of Christ in you.

Long ago, God predicted that light would dispel darkness:

The people walking in darkness have seen a great light; on those living in the land of the shadow of death a light has dawned. You have enlarged the nation and increased their joy; they rejoice before you as people rejoice at the harvest.

Jesus said, "You are the light."
When we remove what's obstructing
His light, nothing in the world can
stop it from being seen.

That prediction came true when you encountered the love and forgiveness of Christ and stepped into the light of His grace. Now He asks you to become a vessel through which His light can shine to the world, shattering its darkness.

Jesus wouldn't have said we are the light of the world if we couldn't *be* the light of the world. The trouble is that we have forgotten what that means—or we never learned it in the first place. We are not just "meant" to be light. Light is who we *are*. Jesus didn't say, "You *can* be the light," but

"You *are* the light." That means His light is already inside us. When we remove what's obstructing His light, nothing in the world can stop it from being seen.

Remember—your *life* is the message. As St. Francis of Assisi said:

> "Preach the Gospel at all times.
> If necessary, use words."

Shine: make em wonder what you got
Make em wish that they were not
On the outside looking bored
Shine, let it shine before all men
Let em see good works and then
Let em glorify the Lord

"Shine"
Going Public, Shine: The Hits

Nothing is wonderful except the abnormal and nothing is abnormal until we have grasped the norm.

—C. S. Lewis

Part II

Living in an Upside-Down Kingdom

The secret of the kingdom of God has been given to you.

—Mark 4:11

And every generation's got
The fearless few who can't be bought
They don't take polls or look around
They act on truth, and then they stand their
ground

Come up and see the world stripped bare
The free indeed
They breathe a rarified air...

Come up and see the big man's boss
The mind clears out when you're taking up
the cross
Yeah, his burden's easy
No, it don't chafe
It's God's safe harbor
Why play it safe?

"Cornelius"
Thrive

*Do not worry, saying, "What shall we eat?"
or "What shall we drink?" or "What shall
we wear?" For the pagans run after all these
things, and your heavenly Father knows that
you need them. But seek first his kingdom
and his righteousness, and all these things
will be given to you as well.*

—Matthew 6:31–33

> Devotion to what is wrong is complex and admits
> of infinite variations.
> —Seneca

You are alone in the house and sound asleep. Slowly you come to consciousness. There's a strange scent in the air. Suddenly, you realize you are smelling smoke. Jumping out of bed, you run to the door, but it's too hot to touch, and you can see the glow of fire from underneath it. To escape the flames, you'll have to climb out the window. Everything you own will soon be burned up in the fire. You can carry only one thing with you—your prized possession.

What would you save?

Wake-Up Call

There are things in life we take for granted until we risk losing them. That truth hit all of us one night when we were celebrating Peter and Summer's tenth anniversary. Everyone at the table was very aware of how God had brought them through some hard times in their relationship and had blessed them with the love and friendship they enjoy today. Partway through the meal, Erica, Jody's wife, realized that she needed to go and buy more formula for their beautiful one-month-old girl, Bethany. She took the baby with her as she went on this routine errand. It wasn't long until Jody received a frantic phone call. Bethany had stopped breathing. For fifteen minutes, Erica did CPR until their precious baby could be rushed to the hospital. In a moment's time, our joy turned to sorrow. Not knowing what would happen, all we could do was be there for Jody and his family at the hospital and pray hard. Jody describes the impact this crisis had on his life:

Bethany's situation has really shown me that it's one thing to have your ministry and the work that you are doing, but there are other things we should be giving our attention to. We really got a big wake-up call when Bethany suddenly became ill. One moment, she was a perfectly normal baby, and the next moment, she was in the midst of a fight for her life in intensive care. The doctors gave her absolutely no chance for survival. She was on life support, and as far as they could tell, she was totally unresponsive. We were at Vanderbilt Medical Center, which is an excellent children's hospital, and the entire team of doctors told us to prepare because "this was it." They even asked for advice from the woman who basically invented critical care in the 1950s. She was retired, but they presented the whole case to her just to get her opinion. There wasn't anyone more experienced than this woman, and even she said, "I don't think there's any way she will survive."

It is amazing how clear things became to us at this time. We complicate our lives so much with so many things, and we work so hard to try to accomplish these great things for God or for ourselves. When everything is going well, we usually get caught up in being a little self-centered somehow and focusing on the wrong things. But during this time, I asked myself, "Man, what am I doing with my life? This is crazy! I have to live every moment to the fullest. I have to appreciate every moment of every day. You just don't know what could happen."

From the start, we had many people praying for Bethany—throughout the country and the world. Because of all those prayers, Bethany is still with us today. It was an incredible miracle. She suffered near brain damage and still has a lot of medical issues, and she ended up being in the hospital for over a month, but she's doing great now. She's wonderful; she's the best thing that's ever happened to us.

We have a tendency sometimes to think that if things aren't going very well, maybe something is wrong with us spiritually. The truth of the matter is that, for me, it's been kind of the opposite. It has been the trials and the hardships that have *really* taught me about the character of God, more than when everything seems great. Even though going through what we did with Bethany was stressful in many ways, there was really never a more peaceful, focused time in our lives than when she was in the hospital. That was because God was there, and everything else was pushed aside. We knew exactly what we should be focusing on and what we were to do.

Through Bethany's situation, as well as other events in our lives, we have come to realize how easy it is to get sidetracked from what really matters.

God is well aware that this is a particular problem for the human race. The first man and woman, Adam and Eve, traded their relationship with God in the Garden of Eden for satisfying their own curiosity. Even the nation of Israel—whom God had called to be His special people—rejected Him and His ways. Instead of being "a kingdom of priests" who would represent God to the world, they became conquered subjects of the Roman Empire, squabbling among themselves for what little position and

> The trials and hardships of life are
> what will really teach you about
> the character of God because in
> those hard times, God is there, and
> everything else is pushed aside.

independence they could scrape out of their existence. Before Christ was born, the whole human race was locked into a continual series of bad choices and misplaced priorities.

God's plan was to break into that destructive cycle and provide a way of escape by sending His Son Jesus into the world. But He knew He would first have to do something dramatic to get His people's attention. What did He do? He stopped talking to them.

If you've ever been tuned out by a friend or spouse because he or she wanted to watch television or read a magazine, you'll know why God chose that method. The best way to get people's attention is to make them start to wonder what you were going to say when they first tuned you out.

For hundreds of years, the Israelites had basically been telling God, "Yeah, we already know all that," when He warned them that rejecting Him and going their own way would lead to their own destruction. But they still didn't return to Him.

So for four hundred years before Christ came, God's people didn't hear anything from Him—not one word from one of His prophets. This time period is often called the "years of silence." The Israelites settled into an unhappy existence under the Romans as they hoped against hope that the Messiah would come and rescue them and restore the kingdom to Israel. Now they desperately wanted to hear a word from God. They wanted to know that God knew all about their situation, that He cared about what they were going through.

Suddenly that silence was broken—first by John the Baptist, whose job was to prepare them for Christ's coming—and then by Jesus Himself. Jesus' earthly ministry began with this wake-up call for God's people:

The kingdom of God is near. Repent and believe the good news!

The Israelites were certainly ready for God to speak again. But were they ready for what He had to say?

All during His ministry, Jesus drove home the message that the most priceless possession any human being could have was God and His kingdom. That wasn't just a message for the Israelites; it was a message for all people of all time. Our wake-up call is to recognize the precious gift God has given us before we waste our lives on lesser things that won't last. Jesus said,

> The kingdom of heaven is like treasure hidden in a field. When a man found it, he hid it again, and then in his joy went and sold all he had and bought that field.

> Again, the kingdom of heaven is like a merchant looking for fine pearls. When he found one of great value, he went away and sold everything he had and bought it.

Jesus spoke of the kingdom of God or the kingdom of heaven—two terms that mean the same thing—over *eighty-five* times in the Gospel accounts, while He mentioned the church by name only twice. Important as the church is, it is part of the larger kingdom of God, which Jesus spent His entire ministry focusing on.

The Gospel of the Kingdom

The Bible very specifically tells us that Jesus' message was not just the Gospel but "the gospel of the kingdom."

When we speak of the Gospel today, we usually mean the message of salvation. Salvation is certainly a crucial aspect of the kingdom, but the kingdom encompasses everything that belongs to God, as well as everything He is doing in heaven and on earth.

The word *kingdom* comes from two words: *king*, which refers to the ultimate source and authority of something, and *dom*, which means dominion, realm, or jurisdiction. Therefore, the kingdom of God is the entire territory of God's authority, reign, and power.

> During his ministry, Jesus drove home the message that the most priceless possession any human being could have was God and His kingdom.

King David said,

Yours, O LORD, is the greatness and the power and the glory and the majesty and the splendor, for everything in heaven and earth is yours. Yours, O LORD, is the kingdom; you are exalted as head over all.

Jesus echoed these words in the Lord's Prayer, when He said, "Your kingdom come. Your will be done on earth as it is in heaven," and "For Yours is the kingdom and the power and the glory forever. Amen."

When Jesus announced that the kingdom of God was near, it was not just rhetoric. He proved the nearness and presence of God by exhibiting power over disease and demons. The Scripture says, "Jesus went through all the towns and villages, teaching in their synagogues, preaching the good news of the kingdom and healing every disease and sickness."

Jesus constantly preached that the kingdom of God had come to earth. It had come in the form of the King Himself—the Word made flesh. The New Testament tells us that the sign the kingdom had truly come was that people who were suffering and who were beyond any human help were healed and delivered by God Himself.

When Jesus sent out His twelve disciples to minister to the people, He instructed them to preach the same thing He was preaching and to do the same thing He was doing: "He gave them power and authority to drive out all demons and to cure diseases, and he sent them out to preach the kingdom of God and to heal the sick." They were functioning in realms of power and authority, which are kingdom issues. Jesus later sent out seventy other disciples with the same mission.

The message of the kingdom continued to be central even after Jesus' death and resurrection. The Acts of the Apostles tells us that from the time Jesus was resurrected to the time He ascended into heaven, His major theme was the kingdom:

After his suffering, he showed himself to these men and gave many convincing proofs that he was alive. He appeared to them over a period of forty days and spoke about the kingdom of God.

Jesus told His followers they were to teach others about the kingdom until He returned to earth in glory: "And this gospel of the kingdom will be preached in the whole world as a testimony to all nations, and then the end will come."

The disciples took this commission seriously. The message of the early church was definitely a kingdom message. In the book of Acts, we read that Paul, Barnabas, and Philip, among others, preached the kingdom. In fact, the book of Acts closes with Paul, at the end of his life, teaching daily on the principles of the kingdom of God.

"Your Kingdom Come, Your Will Be Done"

The wake-up call that God gave humanity after thousands of years of human rebellion and four hundred years of silence echoed through Jesus' ministry and the early church, and it still echoes today. The kingdom of God is beyond a doubt the central theme of Scripture. It is the framework, or paradigm, that guides our understanding of everything else in life.

Probably the greatest proof of the centrality of the kingdom is Jesus' command in the Sermon on the Mount: "But seek first [God's] kingdom and his righteousness, and all these things will be given to you as well."

Do not worry about your life, what you will eat or drink; or about your body, what you will wear. Is not life more important than food, and the body more important than clothes? Look at the birds of the air; they do not sow or reap or store away in barns, and yet your heavenly Father feeds them. Are you not much more valuable than they? Who of you by worrying can add a single hour to his life? And why do you worry about clothes? See how the lilies of the field grow. They do not labor or spin. Yet I tell you that not even Solomon in all his splendor

> The kingdom of God is the framework, or paradigm, that guides our understanding of everything else in life.

was dressed like one of these. If that is how God clothes the grass of the field, which is here today and tomorrow is thrown into the fire, will he not much more clothe you, O you of little faith? So do not worry, saying, "What shall we eat?" or "What shall we drink?" or "What shall we wear?" For the pagans run after all these things, and your heavenly Father knows that you need them. But seek first his kingdom and his righteousness, and all these things will be given to you as well.

Jesus says we are to seek the kingdom above all else, just as He does. Remember that the very first petition Jesus taught His disciples to pray was, "Your kingdom come, your will be done, on earth as it is in heaven." Therefore, our first prayer to God, and our first concern in all that we are and do, should be the kingdom.

The Essence of the Kingdom

Many of Jesus' parables tell us what the kingdom is and how to obtain it. Here is one of the most important, according to Jesus Himself:

> Our first prayer to God, and our first concern in all that we are and do, should be the kingdom.

Listen! A farmer went out to sow his seed. As he was scattering the seed, some fell along the path, and the birds came and ate it up. Some fell on rocky places, where it did not have much soil. It sprang up quickly, because the soil was shallow. But when the sun came up, the plants were scorched, and they withered because they had no root. Other seed fell among thorns, which grew up and choked the plants, so that they did not bear grain. Still other seed fell on good soil. It came up, grew and produced a crop, multiplying thirty, sixty, or even a hundred times.

Jesus ended this parable by saying, "He who has ears to hear, let him hear." His disciples and other followers asked Him to interpret the parable. Jesus answered, "The secret of the kingdom of God has been given to you....Don't you understand this parable? How then will you understand any parable?"

Jesus was saying that once we understand the essence of the kingdom, we'll be able to understand its many facets and the deep treasures of its wisdom. This is the meaning of the parable that He gave to His followers:

The farmer sows the word. Some people are like seed along the path, where the word is sown. As soon as they hear it, Satan comes and takes away the word that was sown in them.

In other words, people who are like the seed on the path hardly give themselves an opportunity to hear the Word of God, or they don't try to understand it. They pass by it with barely a glance.

Others, like seed sown on rocky places, hear the word and at once receive it with joy. But since they have no root, they last only a short time. When trouble or persecution comes because of the word, they quickly fall away.

Those who are like the seed on rocky places accept what they hear of God's Word—as long as it makes them feel good. But when responsibility or perseverance is demanded of them, they quickly abandon it.

Still others, like seed sown among thorns, hear the word; but the worries of this life, the deceitfulness of wealth and the desires for other things come in and choke the word, making it unfruitful.

People who are like the seed sown among thorns know the truth of the Word, but they don't absorb it. They are drawn to the things of this world, which smother the Word until it is choked out of their lives, leaving them unchanged and unproductive for God.

Others, like seed sown on good soil, hear the word, accept it, and produce a crop—thirty, sixty or even a hundred times what was sown.

Those who are like the seed sown on good soil hear and understand the Word, take it to heart, and act on it. They have grasped the essence of the kingdom of God and are allowing God to use them to make it grow even more.

Jesus was teaching us that in order to seek first God's kingdom and righteousness, we must:

☀ Hear the Word

☀ Accept and Understand It

☀ Produce a Harvest for the Kingdom

Hear the Word

After Jesus told His disciples, "The secret of the kingdom of God has been given to you," He added,

Do you bring in a lamp to put it under a bowl or a bed? Instead, don't you put it on its stand? For whatever is hidden is meant to be disclosed, and whatever is concealed is meant to be brought out into the open. If anyone has ears to hear, let him hear.

Before Jesus came, the true nature of the kingdom had been kept secret; it had been a mystery until He came and proclaimed it. But now it is revealed through Him.

Jesus spoke all these things to the crowd in parables; he did not say anything to them without using a parable. So was fulfilled what was spoken through the prophet: "I will open my mouth in parables, I will utter things hidden since the creation of the world."

The apostle Paul wrote about the mystery of the kingdom:

I have become [the church's] servant by the commission God gave me to present to you the word of God in its fullness—the mystery that has been kept hidden for ages and generations, but is now disclosed to the saints. To them God has chosen to make known among the Gentiles the glorious riches of this mystery, which is Christ in you, the hope of glory.

The kingdom remained a mystery until Christ came because we never would have imagined that God Himself would come to earth as a man so the world could be reconciled to Him, so "His kingdom could come and His will be done on earth as it is in heaven." But Jesus, the Word made flesh, has revealed the wonderful mystery of the Gospel: When we receive Jesus into our hearts by faith, we obtain righteousness; we receive the kingdom. The life and character of God lives in us. Although we often try to impose standards of behavior on ourselves and others from the outside, Jesus says to us,

The kingdom of God is within you.

This is the message we must have ears to hear. The kingdom of God is "Christ in us, the hope of glory." This secret of the kingdom can be known only through spiritual rebirth: "No one can see the kingdom of God unless he is born again...unless he is born of water and the Spirit." Once we are reborn, the kingdom is ours. Jesus promises us this: "Do not be afraid, little flock, for your Father has been pleased to give you the kingdom."

Good News!

Throughout the Gospels, we are repeatedly told that the coming of this kingdom is good news. It is "good news of *great joy*," as the angels told the shepherds when Christ was born. Jesus said it is such good news that "everyone is pressing into it."

The kingdom of God is like people waiting in line for the gates to open for a blockbuster summer movie or a championship game. Once the gates are opened, everyone pours through them because they can't wait to be a part of it. Under the old covenant, God was not accessible, but the new covenant is the heavenly Father welcoming us with open arms! All those who thought they had no chance of reconciling with God are streaming through the gates of the kingdom. Only through Christ could this be possible.

Because Christ is in us, God is no longer distant and unreachable. His commandments are no longer

> The heavenly Father is welcoming us with open arms! All those who thought they had no chance of reconciling with God are streaming through the gates of the kingdom.

burdensome requirements that we can never fulfill. Instead, His "yoke is easy and burden light." God says, "I will put my laws in their minds and write them on their hearts. I will be their God, and they will be my people."

This good news is as true for our being the light of the world as it is for our being forgiven from sin. We do not have to struggle to be light. When Jesus lives His life through us, the kingdom itself is lived through us and the light of Christ shines to others. If we want to know what this kingdom within us is like, we just look at Jesus. The essence of His nature is the essence of the kingdom:

> Your attitude should be the same as that of Christ Jesus: who, being in very nature God, did not consider equality with God something to be grasped, but made himself nothing, taking the very nature of a servant, being made in human likeness. And being found in appearance as a man, he humbled himself and became obedient to death—even death on a cross! Therefore God exalted him to the highest place and gave him the name that is above every name, that at the name of Jesus every knee should bow, in heaven and on earth and under the earth, and every tongue confess that Jesus Christ is Lord, to the glory of God the Father.

It's a mind-boggling concept, isn't it? God becoming a servant? God becoming a man, entering the harsh environment of the fallen world as one of us? The nature of His kingdom is upside down from anything we would *imagine*—let alone *do*.

This remarkable passage shows us that when Jesus took the nature of a servant, it was not just a one-time decision—it was an ongoing one. As God, He made Himself nothing, taking the very nature of a servant; and as man, He humbled Himself every day of His life on earth until His ultimate obedience on the cross. It was a choice He continually made.

He asks us to make the same daily choice. As we yield to the life of Christ within us, we choose to take on this attitude of serving others, and we renew this commitment every day. Jesus said, "If anyone would come after me, he must deny himself and take up his cross and follow me."

Donald B. Kraybill, in his book, *The Upside-Down Kingdom*, writes:

> In the upside-down kingdom greatness isn't measured by how much power we exercise over others. Upside-down prestige isn't calculated by our rank on the social ladder. In God's inverted kingdom, greatness is determined by our willingness to serve. Service to others is the yardstick of status in the new kingdom.

Our God is nothing like the supposed gods of ancient times, whom people served out of fear and intimidation. He is not like our gods of status and success today, who rule us through a similar method. These gods demand homage. They would never humble themselves to serve us! Yet our God stooped from His position of power and glory not only to redeem us, but also to show us the way to true life. He doesn't ask us to do anything that He is not also willing to do.

The other gods were strong; but Thou wast weak;
They rode, but Thou didst stumble to a throne;
But to our wounds only God's wounds can speak,
And not a god has wounds but Thou alone.
—Edward Shillito

The Son of God allowed Himself to become weak and "stumbled" to the throne through His death on the cross. Only Christ's experience on earth can speak to our own human condition. Christ really knows what it is to be one of us. When we truly understand what it meant for Christ to take on human form and empty Himself completely for our sakes, then we have really *heard* the Word of the Gospel of the kingdom.

Jesus gave us a vivid picture of this truth when He said that we can enter the kingdom only if we have the humility of a child. "I tell you the truth, anyone who will not receive the kingdom of God like a little child will never enter it." He contrasted the image of a child with the image of a powerful and rich man:

As a man, Jesus humbled Himself
every day of His life on earth.
It was a choice He continually
made. He asks us to make the
same choice daily.

I tell you the truth, it is hard for a rich man to enter the kingdom of heaven. Again I tell you, it is easier for a camel to go through the eye of a needle than for a rich man to enter the kingdom of God.

When we hear these words of Christ, we realize that we're living in a kingdom unlike any of the kingdoms of this world. Who do we normally think of as more powerful and influential—a multimillionaire or a kindergartner? Jesus' disciples asked Him who would be greatest in the kingdom of heaven. That was the wrong question. The question should have been, "Will I serve others and welcome them in Christ's name?" Jesus replied, "Whoever humbles himself like this child is the greatest in the kingdom of heaven."

> Jesus' disciples asked Him who would be greatest in the kingdom of heaven. The question should have been, "Will I serve others?"

The nature of the kingdom that our Father has been pleased to give us is this: love and selflessness. The words of Jesus come to us gently but with urgency:

> Whoever wants to save his life will lose it, but whoever loses his life for me and for the gospel will save it.

This is often a hard concept for us to accept, because of its upside-down nature. Our whole culture emphasizes doing things through our own efforts. We're told, "You can do it! If you follow this five-step program, you can be this or do that. It's all within your power." That is the message we are continually bombarded with. Sometimes it's subtle, and sometimes it's very blatant. On the surface, it seems like a positive message. But it's actually the reverse of what the Scripture says: "I can do all things through Christ who strengthens me." It doesn't say "through me." It says "through Christ." The world says we're supposed to be strong, independent, and self-sufficient. Yet God says if we want to be really strong, we must give our lives over to Him and let Him live His life through us. A life of service and love for others can't be accomplished through a five-step method. It must be lived out daily.

> A life of service and love for others can't be accomplished through a five-step method. It must be lived out daily.

Having some experience in this matter, we know that it can be a tough thing for males to release control of their lives to God. It is very tough, especially for a young man, to say to anybody, "You're the Lord over my life," because he wants to feel strong. Males in their teens think they are indestructible. They're going to live forever and conquer the world. It's very difficult and humbling for them to say to another Entity—as great and as powerful and as magnificent as the Creator is—"You're in control."

Many of us still hold on to a desire for self-preservation—we want to hold on to our way of doing things rather than accepting the way of surrender to Christ. We all have that thing inside us that the Bible calls the "old man" or the sin nature, which still entices us to promote ourselves, even in small ways. If we listen to its urgings, our faith will not be about losing ourselves in order to gain Christ; we will have missed the true message of the kingdom, and our light will be blocked. The people who really make a difference—and they seem to be found only in limited numbers—are those who have truly lost themselves, who have moved through the eye of the needle.

When Jesus said, "It is easier for a camel to go through the eye of a needle than for a rich man to enter the kingdom of God," He was describing someone who refuses to loosen his grip on the riches of this earth in order to live for the kingdom. The "rich man" doesn't necessarily have to be someone who is wealthy. He could be someone who wants to be rich in making a name for himself, or someone who wants to be rich in having all the latest technology, or someone who wants to be rich in being admired as intelligent, athletic, or beautiful.

The key to real riches is losing yourself—your opinions, your way of doing things, and perhaps your own goals—for the sake of Christ. This does not mean just losing your life, but losing it *for the sake of Christ and the Gospel of the kingdom.* There is a significant difference. As the apostle Paul said, "Submit to one another out of reverence for Christ." Many people are afraid of loss, but surrender to Christ is a different kind of loss. In the upside-down kingdom, temporary loss for Christ's sake equals eternal—and exponential—gain. We will receive a rich reward both now and in eternity. The apostle Paul said, "The kingdom of God is...righteousness, peace and joy in the Holy Spirit, because anyone who serves Christ in this way is pleasing to God and approved by men."

Accept the Word

After we hear the Word—that is, after we understand the true nature of the kingdom—we must fully accept it. If we make hearing the truth our only goal, we will be in danger of having that truth choked out of our lives, so that it does not bear any fruit. God says that those whose hearts become hard to His Word will be "ever hearing, but never understanding." Jesus tells us how we can accept the Word into our lives so it can be planted—and ultimately reap a harvest for the kingdom. He said, "*Repent, for the kingdom of heaven is near.*"

Although repentance obviously involves asking forgiveness for sin and receiving salvation, there is even more to it than that. The Greek word that we translate as *repent* means "to think differently" or "to change one's mind or purpose." The Phillips Bible version translates it as "Change your hearts and minds," and the New Century Bible translates it as "Change your hearts and lives." Another definition of *repentance* is "turning around and going in the opposite direction than you have been going."

Changing our thinking—our hearts and lives—is exactly where we need to start in order to "be the change we want to see" in the world. It is so easy to hold on to old patterns of thinking and living that do not reflect the attitude of Christ. As the quote by Seneca at the beginning of this section says, there are many ways we can become devoted to what is false, without our realizing it. Solomon emphasized this point in Proverbs: "There is a way that seems right to a man, but in the end it leads to death." But we must fully embrace kingdom thinking if we are to have the servant heart of Jesus. Part of humbling ourselves for the sake of Christ is recognizing that our natural mind-set, which is based on the fallen nature, needs to be totally transformed:

> "For my thoughts are not your thoughts, neither are your ways my ways," declares the LORD. "As the heavens are higher than the earth, so are my ways higher than your ways and my thoughts than your thoughts."

There are many things that seem right on the surface but don't promote the kingdom or God's best plan for us. Solomon said, "Though God has made men upright, each has turned away to follow his own downward road." C. S. Lewis put it this way: "There is but one good; that is God. Everything else is good when it looks to Him and bad when it turns from Him."

During storms or extremely dense fog, pilots can become disoriented and fly their planes right into the ground. They don't realize they are flying in the wrong direction because either they don't have any instruments or their instruments are giving them the wrong information. A similar thing happens to people who live without any objective instruments they can rely on to guide them. When these people try to navigate through life's difficulties, they wreck their lives. The principles of the kingdom give us the objective instruments we need to live. They set us upright and on the correct course, even when life's storms prevent us from seeing very far into the future.

The world has its own version of reality, but true reality is the way God has ordered and established heaven and earth and caused them to work. If we want to know what is authentic, we have to follow the ways of the kingdom. The upside-down kingdom calls us to reject the spirit of the world and accept the Spirit of Truth. Jesus said, "What is highly valued among men is detestable in God's sight." The world's thinking is corruptible—it's not lasting because it's not based on truth. But God is eternal, and neither He nor His words are corruptible. He is the only true reality.

Changing our thinking does not mean reading a few Bible verses every day, but a genuine *commitment* to an entirely new way of looking at our priorities, attitudes, and actions. It is a paradigm shift. The way we normally think and reason often causes us to strive and struggle with ourselves and others—and God. But God says to us, in effect, "If you think in the kingdom way, things will fall into place, because they will be in alignment with My heart and will. All the pieces will fit into the puzzle. There won't be one little piece that you try to jam into place to try to make it fit. You will find perspective for your entire life—past, present, and future." Jesus said, "If you hold to my teaching, you are really my disciples. Then you will know the truth, and the truth will set you free."

In order to learn to think differently, we must re-center our minds, remembering that change doesn't come from our own internal resources or ideas, but from Christ Himself, who lives within us.

It's important for us to start at the beginning and rethink everything according to kingdom principles, because if we try to add God's reality to our own reality, the two will never fit together and we will likely set aside God's reality. Jesus told two parables that give us a picture of this condition:

No one sews a patch of unshrunk cloth on an old garment, for the patch will pull away from the garment, making the tear worse. Neither do men pour new wine into old wineskins. If they do, the skins will burst, the wine will run out and the wineskins will be ruined. No, they pour new wine into new wineskins, and both are preserved.

So Christ's word to us is, in effect: "Repent! Give your perspective a radical overhaul so you can enter fully into the life and joy of the kingdom." The apostle Peter told the

Israelites, "Repent, then, and turn to God, so that your sins may be wiped out, that times of refreshing may come from the Lord."

Repentance not only enables us to receive the Good News, but also ushers in times of refreshing! Our spirits, souls, and minds will be renewed as we understand and accept God's thoughts and ways.

Wisdom from the Upside-Down Kingdom

One of Jesus' first teachings, called the Sermon on the Mount, is filled with sayings that epitomize the upside-down kingdom. The beginning part of this teaching is called the Beatitudes, which show us what a person is like when he is living in and for the kingdom.

Actually, the kingdom is right side up. It is *we* who are upside-down because we are used to thinking according to the "old man." But when we accept and enter into these truths, the Spirit and life of Christ will shine clearly through us.

"The Beatitudes"
Matthew 5:3-12
The Sermon on the Mount

Blessed are the poor in spirit, for theirs is the kingdom of heaven.

Blessed are those who mourn, for they will be comforted.

Blessed are the meek, for they will inherit the earth.

Blessed are those who hunger and thirst for righteousness, for they will be filled.

Blessed are the merciful, for they will be shown mercy.

Blessed are the pure in heart, for they will see God.

Blessed are the peacemakers, for they will be called sons of God.

Blessed are those who are persecuted because of righteousness, for theirs is the kingdom of heaven.

Blessed are you when people insult you, persecute you and falsely say all kinds of evil against you because of me.

Rejoice and be glad, because great is your reward in heaven, for in the same way they persecuted the prophets who were before you.

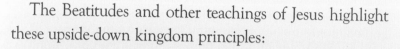

The Beatitudes and other teachings of Jesus highlight these upside-down kingdom principles:

If you want to find your life, you have to lose your life.

Love your enemies; do good to those who hate you.

When you are struck, don't retaliate.

When you are offended, forgive.

It is more blessed to give than to receive.

It is the poor in spirit, not the rich in spirit, who are blessed.

It is the peacemakers, not the victorious debaters, who have God's blessing.

Do you want to be exalted? Then humble yourself.

Do you want to be great? Then be the servant of all.

Jesus said, "Whoever practices and teaches these commands will be called great in the kingdom of heaven." These principles define the servant nature of Christ—who brings love where there is hatred, forgiveness where there is bitterness, and reconciliation where there is estrangement. He calls us to follow His example of breaking the cycle of sin and death in the world by our attitudes and actions of love.

The things that the world sees as weak are the things that will bring us true spiritual strength. For example, Jesus said,

"Blessed are the poor in spirit." If you're poor in anything, it means you don't have enough of it. To be "poor in spirit" shows you recognize you need the true Spirit filling your life. This acknowledgment is essential to receiving the blessings God wants to give you. The world thinks we're well off when we don't have any needs, but Jesus said, in essence, "You're blessed when you have a need and you *know* it, because God can then meet that need."

> The world thinks we're well off
> when we don't have any needs. But
> Jesus said we're blessed when we
> have needs and realize it because
> then God can meet those needs.

What it means to serve in an upside-down kingdom was mystifying at first to those in Jesus' day, because the secret of the kingdom was being revealed to them for the first time. The Beatitudes seemed backward to the disciples and others who listened to Christ teach. Some thought He was going to start an earthly revolution against the Romans, but here He was saying things like, "Blessed are the peacemakers." Jesus always seemed to start out with about 5,000 people gathered around Him, but after they had listened to Him speak for a while, He often ended up with just the original Twelve (and some of *them* may have been having second thoughts!).

Kingdom living is a truly radical overhaul of our lives. That is why we should have patience with ourselves as these kingdom secrets are unfolding to us, remembering that we have been trained all our lives to think in the opposite way. In the end, understanding and accepting what it means to lose our lives for Christ's sake can be accomplished only by the work of God's Holy Spirit. We need to ask Him to help us understand what Jesus' words mean for our own lives. We should prepare ourselves to receive God's truth by asking the Spirit to reveal it to us.

> Understanding and accepting what it means to lose our lives for Christ's sake can be accomplished only by the work of God's Holy Spirit.

As Jesus said, "When he, the Spirit of truth, comes, he will guide you into all truth."

Refine Your Mind

Renewing our minds with the truths of the upside-down kingdom is a matter of taking in God's Word every day and saying, "I repent and commit to believing God's truth rather than the world's thinking or my own ideas." It's a continual process that enables His Word to permeate our spirits and lives, like the example Jesus gave of the "yeast that a woman took and mixed into a large amount of flour until it worked all through the dough."

The apostle Paul talked about "working out our salvation with fear and trembling." We've taken his words to mean, "Work out how to be saved." But they mean much more than that. His words were addressed to believers, and his emphasis was on "work out *your* salvation with fear and trembling." Our salvation is a very sacred thing that is not to be taken lightly. It is to be taken reverently and with great gratitude. That is why we must say to ourselves, "I am saved. I believe. Now, what is my faith all about? How do I go about living it?" These are the questions that lead us to the secret of the kingdom and surrendering to the life of Christ within us so we can become strong in Him.

Produce a Harvest for the Kingdom

Jesus said that when the Word of God falls on good soil in our lives, not only do we hear and accept it, but we also produce a harvest for the kingdom as it matures within us. We will recognize the presence of the kingdom by the fruit it produces. Jesus was saying that growth is a natural aspect of the kingdom. Lack of growth is an indication that something is not right. Jesus made this point strongly in the parable of the barren fig tree:

> A man had a fig tree, planted in his vineyard, and he went to look for fruit on it, but did not find any. So he said to the man who took care of the vineyard, "For three years now I've been coming to look for fruit on this fig tree and haven't found any. Cut it

down! Why should it use up the soil?" "Sir," the man replied, "leave it alone for one more year, and I'll dig around it and fertilize it. If it bears fruit next year, fine! If not, then cut it down."

At another time, Jesus said, "The kingdom of God will be...given to a people who will produce its fruit." The apostle Paul said that he preached to all people "that they should repent and turn to God and prove their repentance by their deeds." Our harvest for the kingdom will be proof that our lives have truly been transformed by the renewing of our minds in Christ and have produced eternal spiritual fruit. Work in the harvest fields of the kingdom is not an obligation, but a healthy outgrowth of our kingdom thinking and living.

The fruit we are to harvest for the kingdom is the character of Christ in our own lives, our service for God, and the reproduction of the life of Christ in others as we live out the Gospel of the kingdom. We are to tell this mystery to the world—to those who have ears to hear.

It is our commitment to Christ and to hearing and accepting His Word that will reap this harvest. Whatever God has given us—gifts, talents, opportunities—we need to use for Him, trusting Him to bring kingdom results. As we are faithful, God will bring the increase.

A good illustration of this kingdom principle is the way God led Jeff to become a member of the band. Here is his story:

My dad was a pastor, and I grew up in a Christian family, but I was very frustrated with my life. I was going to college, studying public relations, planning on taking an internship at Warner Brothers, and doing all these things, but I wasn't sure what God wanted me to do. I wanted to do what He wanted me to do, but nothing was happening, so I thought that I would plan out my own life. If God decided to do anything different, then that would be great, but in the meantime, I was going to do what I was going to do.

I had been playing music in church for six or seven years. I was very faithful in the music ministry, but it was a *real* struggle for me, because I didn't really enjoy playing at church. I was the only young person involved in it, and it wasn't considered "cool." No one else in the church knew how to play the piano, so for years I was up there leading the praise and worship with my mom, who was the music director. I was a teenage kid with all these dreams of wanting to do things with my music—maybe play in a band—but feeling as if my life was going nowhere.

One morning, I was playing the piano in church, and I remember saying to God, "Please, whatever You want me to do, just use me, whether I stay here or go somewhere else. But if I'm going to stay here, please give me a fresh perspective on things, because I'm feeling burned out." It probably sounds funny now, but I was kind of burned out at eighteen years old. High school was over, college would be over in a few years, and at the time I felt, "What is left?"

Within three weeks of praying that prayer, through a remarkable turn of events, I had left college and was on the road, traveling across America, playing with the band. It was the most amazing answer to prayer that I've ever experienced in my life. I'll never forget it, because it was such a powerful thing.

That was a pretty dramatic experience, but what I learned from it was to be faithful in the little things, to be faithful in whatever you do. Maybe not everyone is going to be in a band, but in God's eyes, if you turn your life over to Him, He'll use you. He'll put you where He wants you to be.

As we seek to serve the kingdom, God will put us where He wants us to be. We have only a certain amount of time, energy, and attention to give to our lives. Therefore, we have a choice of using what we have for selfish purposes or for kingdom purposes. Our choice will have eternal ramifications, as the parable of the talents, or minas, reveals:

A man of noble birth went to a distant country to have himself appointed king and then to return.

So he called ten of his servants and gave them ten minas. "Put this money to work," he said, "until I come back." But his subjects hated him and sent a delegation after him to say, "We don't want this man to be our king." He was made king, however, and returned home. Then he sent for the servants to whom he had given the money, in order to find out what they had gained with it. The first one came and said, "Sir, your mina has earned ten more." "Well done, my good servant!" his master replied. "Because you have been trustworthy in a very small matter, take charge of ten cities." The second came and said, "Sir, your mina has earned five more." His master answered, "You take charge of five cities." Then another servant came and said, "Sir, here is your mina; I have kept it laid away in a piece of cloth. I was afraid of you, because you are a hard man. You take out what you did not put in and reap what you did not sow." His master replied, "I will judge you by your own words, you wicked servant! You knew, did you, that I am a hard man, taking out what I did not put in, and reaping what I did not sow? Why then didn't you put my money on deposit, so that when I came back, I could have collected it with interest?" Then he said to those standing by, "Take his mina away from him and give it to the one who has ten minas." "Sir," they said, "he already has ten!" He replied, "I tell you that to everyone who has, more will be given, but as for the one who has nothing, even what he has will be taken away."

God has given us a serious responsibility. Our lives have great meaning and purpose because God has asked us to produce fruit for His kingdom. When we get sidetracked from His purposes, we start to think we can live our lives any way we want to. However, we will be held accountable for what we have done with what we have been given.

> We will be held accountable for what we have done with what we have been given.

Before we start to become anxious about this responsibility, we must remember the secret of the kingdom, because that is also the secret to the harvest: *Christ in us.* The apostle Paul wrote, "I have been crucified with Christ and I no longer live, but Christ lives in me. The life I live in the body, I live by faith in the Son of God, who loved me and gave himself for me." The pressure and weight we often feel about having to "produce for God" is taken away as we seek Christ first. This doesn't mean that we aren't to work hard; we are to be diligent in our service. Rather, it means that we aren't to feel as if we have to do these things in our own strength. This is our promise: "I can do all things *through Christ* who strengthens me." When we seek the kingdom first, we will automatically become a light to the world.

The Heart of the Harvester

When we try to serve God in our own strength, the focus turns from Christ to ourselves, and we revert back to our old self-absorbed ways. Sometimes we forget the ultimate reason for the harvest—the multitudes of people in this world who are lost without God. Our heavenly Father holds them in His heart, and He longs to bring them into His kingdom. Jesus manifested the same longing:

> When [Jesus] saw the crowds, he had compassion on them, because they were harassed and helpless, like sheep without a shepherd. Then he said to his disciples, "The harvest is plentiful but the workers are few. Ask the Lord of the harvest, therefore, to send out workers into his harvest field."

The Gospel has always been "good news of great joy that will be for *all* the people." When we earnestly ask the Lord of the harvest to send out workers, we will get excited about the work ourselves. The same message we have received is the message they must hear through us: "The time has come....The kingdom of God is near. Repent and believe the good news!"

How we *think* people will respond, or how they actually *do* respond, should not stop us from being the light of the world. Jesus explained that the harvest field will include both good crops and weeds. Only in the end will Christ "separate the sheep from the goats"—but that is not for us to decide. We are called to be His witnesses to the whole world. It is our job to be faithful, and God will reap the harvest among those who have ears to hear.

> The kingdom of heaven is like a man who sowed good seed in his field. But while everyone was sleeping, his enemy came and sowed weeds among the wheat, and went away. When the wheat sprouted and formed heads, then the weeds also appeared. The owner's servants came to him and said, "Sir, didn't you sow good seed in your field? Where then did the weeds come from?" "An enemy did this," he replied. The servants asked him, "Do you want us to go and pull them up?" "No," he answered, "because while you are pulling the weeds, you may root up the wheat with them. Let both grow together until the harvest. At that time I will tell the harvesters: First collect the weeds and tie them in bundles to be burned; then gather the wheat and bring it into my barn."

Jesus died for all, though all do not accept His sacrifice on their behalf. As workers in the harvest field, we must trust God to reveal the mystery of the kingdom to those who are willing to hear. One thing we can be sure of: They will hear that message most clearly when we are not just talking about the Christian life but are actually living a life that reflects the nature of Christ. When we demonstrate love and servanthood to our families, friends, and neighbors; to strangers we meet; and to our enemies, the mystery of the kingdom will be manifested to them.

Whenever we become discouraged during our harvesting, we should remember this: It is only the Spirit of Christ who can reveal the secrets of God's Word to us, and the same is true for those who have not yet entered the kingdom. We must trust that the Holy Spirit not only will give us power to go out into the harvest field, but also will bring in the harvest.

> People will hear the message of the kingdom most clearly when we are not just talking about the Christian life but are actually living a life that reflects the nature of Christ.

What's Our Motivation?

The truth is in,
The proof is when,
You hear your heart start asking,
"What's my motivation?"

Ultimately, the question we must ask ourselves is, What's our motivation for living? Are we giving lip service to the kingdom—or are we really living for it? Do we value what Christ values? Do we share His priorities, or are we seeking to fulfill selfish goals? Sometimes we think that as long as we're not living in obvious sin, we're doing all right by God's standards. But Christ says, "Seek *first* the kingdom." Anything less than that could be second best or twenty-second best, but it still isn't God's best for us.

Even within the realm of the church, we can have misplaced priorities. All biblical truths, unless they are centered on the kingdom of God, inevitably become man-centered. If we were to list the truths of the Bible, we would include salvation, faith, prayer, and many others. Although it's good to highlight certain truths, if we focus on only one of them while neglecting the others, if we let that truth become the center of our lives—rather than the kingdom—we will lose our spiritual balance. This is something every Christian, as well as every church and denomination, has to guard against.

For example, if you put faith at the center of everything you understand about truth, ultimately you end up using faith primarily for yourself rather than for God. Faith becomes about your needs rather than kingdom needs. Prayer, praise and worship, Bible study, and the gifts of the Spirit can all become man-centered. There are times when we can become so involved in the gifts that we forget they were not given for our private enjoyment; they were given so the church could be built up and the kingdom of God could grow. One of Jesus' parables emphasizes that the kingdom is not meant to flourish on its own, but to uphold and sustain others:

The kingdom of heaven is like a mustard seed, which a man took and planted in his field. Though it is the smallest of all your seeds, yet when it grows, it is the largest of garden plants and becomes a tree, so that the birds of the air come and perch in its branches.

Maybe the reason Jesus talked about the kingdom much more than about the church was so that we wouldn't focus only on ourselves, but on what God is seeking to accomplish for His kingdom in this world. When we think primarily about our own needs, we are ripe for that "us versus them" thinking that shuts out the world instead of encouraging us to reach out to it.

This was true even of Jesus' disciples, who for a long time thought He was preparing for a political kingdom. Even after His resurrection, they seemed to expect this to happen. The Bible tells us,

[Jesus] showed himself to these men and gave many convincing proofs that he was alive. He appeared to them over a period of forty days and spoke about the kingdom of God. On one occasion, while he was eating with them, he gave them this command: "Do not leave Jerusalem, but wait for the gift my Father promised, which you have heard me speak about. For John baptized with water, but in a few days you will be baptized with the Holy Spirit." So when they met together, they asked him, "Lord, are you at this time going to restore the kingdom to Israel?" He said to them: "It is not for you to know the times or dates the Father has set by his own authority. But you will receive power when the Holy Spirit comes on you; and you will be my witnesses in Jerusalem, and in all Judea and Samaria, and to the ends of the earth."

The disciples were waiting for the kingdom of Israel to be restored to what it had been in its glory days. They were waiting for a new King David. They believed that Jesus was who He said He was, but it is obvious that His idea of the kingdom and their idea of it were two different

> The disciples believed that
> Jesus was who He said He was,
> but it is obvious that His idea
> of the kingdom and their idea of
> it were two different things.

things. They wanted a kingdom that would fit their own idea of the way things should be.

Because the disciples misunderstood the nature of the kingdom, their perspective became distorted. They wanted the Good News only for themselves and weren't thinking of the Gentiles' need to be reconciled to God. At one point, the mother of James and John asked Jesus if her sons could sit next to Him when He sat on His throne in the kingdom. The other disciples resented this request. However, Jesus' answer, once again, was, "Whoever wants to become great among you must be your servant, and whoever wants to be first must be your slave—just as the Son of Man did not come to be served, but to serve, and to give his life as a ransom for many."

"Lord, I'll Follow You, But..."

When we begin to ask ourselves the difficult question of whether or not we are really seeking first the kingdom, the temptation is to make excuses for ourselves. Jesus encountered a number of people who said they wanted to follow Him—but not yet.

> Jesus knows people's hearts. He knows there is always another excuse we can give for not putting His kingdom first.

[Jesus] said to another man, "Follow me." But the man replied, "Lord, first let me go and bury my father." Jesus said to him, "Let the dead bury their own dead, but you go and proclaim the kingdom of God." Still another said, "I will follow you, Lord; but first let me go back and say good-by to my family." Jesus replied, "No one who puts his hand to the plow and looks back is fit for service in the kingdom of God."

On the surface, these seem like some legitimate excuses. However, Jesus knows people's hearts, and there was more going on in these people's lives than meets the eye. Jesus isn't saying we should neglect our families; He is saying there is always another excuse we can give for not putting His kingdom first. The parable of the great banquet clearly illustrates this:

A certain man was preparing a great banquet and invited many guests. At the time of the banquet he sent his servant to tell those who had been invited, "Come, for everything is now ready." But they all alike began to make excuses. The first said, "I have just bought a field, and I must go and see it. Please excuse me." Another said, "I have just bought five yoke of oxen, and I'm on my way to try them out. Please excuse me." Still another said, "I just got married, so I can't come." The servant came back and reported this to his master. Then the owner of the house became angry and ordered his servant, "Go out quickly into the streets and alleys of the town and bring in the poor, the crippled, the blind and the lame." "Sir," the servant said, "what you ordered has been done, but there is still room." Then the master told his servant, "Go out to the roads and country lanes and make them come in, so that my house will be full. I tell you, not one of those men who were invited will get a taste of my banquet."

We make similar excuses when God invites us to participate in the life of the kingdom: "I'll serve God when I'm out of school and don't have to use my time studying," or "I'll serve God when my children are older," or "I'll work at a business for a few years and then serve God when I have more money."

We say these things because we misunderstand the nature of the kingdom. We are thinking of certain things we might *do* for God, instead of thinking of what He wants us to *become* in Him. Anyone can commit himself or herself to living in the secret of the kingdom—allowing the life of Christ to shine through us as we decrease and

> We think about certain things we might do for God, instead of focusing on what He wants us to become in Him.

He increases. When we do this, Jesus Himself will enable us to produce a harvest—not in our strength, but in His.

Sometimes we don't seek the kingdom first because we're distracted with life, like the seed sown among the thorns. Many people place a great deal of emphasis on their careers and making money. They worry about them so much that they hardly ever think about God's kingdom. Author Frederick Buechner said, "There are people who use up their entire lives making money so they can enjoy

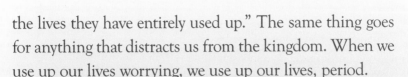

the lives they have entirely used up." The same thing goes for anything that distracts us from the kingdom. When we use up our lives worrying, we use up our lives, period.

Jesus said that God knows we need things like money, jobs, and clothes to wear. But if we focus on them exclusively, we'll never get around to setting kingdom priorities. We'll never have time to help the kingdom grow. We are to trust our heavenly Father to provide for our temporal needs so we can concentrate on eternal issues. Jesus said that when we seek first the kingdom, *all these things will be added unto us.*

When we seek first the kingdom, we have God's promise that all the secondary things will increase as well. All the things we used to worry about will settle themselves. Living in that truth will give us a confidence and peace in life instead of worry and anxiety. Psalm 112 says, "A righteous man will be remembered forever. He will have no fear of bad news; his heart is steadfast, trusting in the LORD." The heart of a righteous man knows that no matter what happens, he can have peace, because God is with him.

Another way to become distracted from kingdom priorities is to allow ourselves to get wrapped up in making a good impression on other people. This happens more often when we are young, but it can be a problem for people of all ages. Young people tend to be very self-absorbed. They're involved in discovering their own identity and dealing with peer pressure: Am I wearing the right clothes, driving the right car, hanging out with the right people?

The world tells us to go along with the crowd. We have to make sure we don't get sidetracked by trying to please people who don't have God's interests at heart. Instead, we must keep God's priorities central in our lives. We constantly have other priorities thrown at us by television and magazines, by what consumerism says we have to be and do to be acceptable to other people. Eternally, those things mean absolutely *nothing*. In one moment, they will all be gone. Then what will we be left with?

Seeking first the kingdom is the only thing that is both lasting and satisfying. When we ignore the call of the kingdom, we often attempt to fill the void with material things. But the latest computer games and movies satisfy only for a certain amount of time before we're looking for the next one to come out. A new car, boat, or sound system won't satisfy us for very long, either. There is a place for many of these things, but they won't fill the deep-down need that only Christ and His kingdom can meet. Whether we realize it or not, we can be fulfilled only by an intimate, ongoing relationship with Christ as we share in His life.

One of the teachers of the law asked Jesus, "Of all the commandments, which is the most important?" Jesus answered,

"Love the Lord your God with all your heart and with all your soul and with all your mind and with all your strength." The second is this: "Love your neighbor as yourself." There is no commandment greater than these.

This is the essence of the kingdom. Loving God with all that we are and loving our neighbors as ourselves are our top two kingdom priorities. Seeking first the kingdom means pre-committing our lives to God—no matter what. In other words, regardless of what happens to us in life, we are already committed to putting God first and serving others in His name, so that we can say to Him, "Whatever You want of me, that's what I want of me."

> Seeking first the kingdom means
> we commit our lives to God—
> no matter what.

The Choice

The choice is ours. We can decide to seek God first. We can truly hunger and thirst for God's righteousness, seek His will for our lives, become who He wants us to be, and reach out to others through the love of Christ.

The alternative is to wait until life causes us to crash and burn, until we have no place else to go, until we're backed into a corner and God has our attention so that

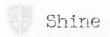

we finally have ears to hear. The only way to find purpose, peace, and fulfillment, the only way to have a life that truly works, is to discover the secret of the upside-down kingdom: "Whoever finds his life will lose it, and whoever loses his life for my sake will find it."

If you make the choice to move forward, we guarantee that you will never be the same.

The Christian ideal has not
been tried and found
wanting. It has been found
difficult; and left untried.

—G. K. Chesterton

I came to a time in my life when the band had three or four gold records and I'd accomplished more than I'd ever imagined I would, like playing in Madison Square Garden. That might not be huge in the world's standards, but I just came from a fishing village in Australia. I'd also made enough money to live on for the rest of my life. But I wasn't satisfied; I didn't have real peace.

It wasn't as if I was always walking around saying, "I've got all this and it doesn't mean anything." But I had used material things as a form of comfort, and suddenly, the vat was full. I'd bought everything that I wanted to buy. There was nothing else that I wanted, so I couldn't use buying things as a source of happiness any longer. Money was an area that I felt had let me down—thank God.

It's the old story. You've heard it all before, but it's still true: Money isn't everything. Someone who has never had money can say, "It's not everything," and they might really know that truth and believe it. However, if you find someone who has had it and who says it, they know what they're talking about, because it's really the truth.

So I had tried everything, all under the name of Jesus, of course, because that's who I thought I was living for. But I finally realized that the center of my will was me, that everything in my life revolved around me. It takes a strong wife to help you see that. Then it takes the grace of God for you to accept it. It was a very hard thing to realize about myself. But it was at that time—probably one of the saddest times of my life—that I wrote the song "Joy" with Steve Taylor. The timing might sound strange, but that's when we find joy—when all our efforts have run out and we have nowhere else to go but to Jesus in surrender. In some ways, I kind of long for that. I don't want to go through that low period again, but one of my prayers has been that God would help me not to forget where I was because it was in that place that I found joy.

It was when I put Christ at the center of my life, and my wife next to Him, that *everything* changed. All of a sudden the dirty water left and the clean spring came in. I had real peace. Where I used to care about getting the right ads in magazines, or giving the right interview, or what people thought of the band, or all these kinds of things, now I have different priorities. I've had a paradigm shift. I'm aiming to please God and my family first. And that has put everything in my life into a new order.

One thing that has really come home to me lately is the meaning of, "Seek first the kingdom of God and His righteousness, and all these things shall be added to you." Matthew 26 talks about how beautiful the lilies of the field are, even though they don't put any effort into it, and how the birds of the air don't stress about where they're going to get their next meal. If they're not concerned, and almighty God provides for them, how much more will He provide for us?

A couple of books have helped me understand these things better: *The Prayer of Jabez*, by Bruce Wilkinson, and also his follow-up book, *Secrets of the Vine*. There is a Scripture that says God wants us to prosper even as our soul prospers. The important thing is not how many records I sell or what kind of car I buy. I believe that God wants those types of blessings for us. If we receive them, that's okay, too. But all the temporal things we put so much emphasis on are just going to be burned up in the end. The Bible says this life is really like a puff of smoke. I don't want to strive and stress and be anxious over a puff of smoke when I have eternity to look forward to. To me, real prosperity means having a good relationship with God and with my wife and children. Those things are eternal.

I also think we have a responsibility as Christians to grow and develop our talents. I don't want God to say to me, on that Day when I stand before Him, "What did you do with that talent I gave you? I gave you this talent and you went and buried it? Depart from Me, you evil, wicked servant!" Instead, I want Him to say, "Great job. Awesome job. You went and developed that one talent into two talents or three talents."

This is what I've learned: Don't despise what God has given you. Don't neglect to develop your gifts. If He's given us something, we have a responsibility to make it grow. That includes our families. The spouse that God has given you is like a talent, in a sense. He has entrusted her or him to you. We can help our spouses and children to become everything God created them to be by praying for them and encouraging them in their gifts and abilities. That means giving them our time. I call this "patio time." Sitting around the patio every night after dinner and giving my family my time and undivided attention.

Driving around, being in a band, and doing all the things people would expect to be glamorous—which are, at times—can be a pretty exciting lifestyle. I won't downplay it. At a certain point in my life, it was something that I was really aspiring to, but now I'm realizing that although it has been great and exciting, it's nothing compared to real life, which is knowing your family well, knowing your neighbors, and becoming the person that God has meant for you to be. That's where real change starts.

I'm in the midst of a process—and it will be a lifelong one—of growing up and asking the Lord to make me the man that *He* wants me to be—not just the person I think I'm supposed to be or that others think I'm supposed to be. My priority is learning how He wants to shape my life and what He wants to do with my life from moment to moment.

All I want is what God wants. I'm realizing that there have been times in my life when I've completely run ahead of the Lord, when I've made plans and done things that weren't necessarily wrong and sinful, but just weren't what He wanted. I didn't really think about what I was doing because I hadn't been giving Him the firstfruits of my day. I hadn't been falling to my knees every day and praying, "Lord, what do You want to show me?"

Now I have a quiet time every day. I'm getting up forty minutes earlier than I used to and having a good prayer time. That's so important. Before, my prayer times were more sporadic. I used to think, "If I can find the time to pray, I will, but not today. I'm too busy," or "I'm so tired, I think I need to sleep. Maybe I'll pray later in the afternoon." And often I would pray in the afternoon, but there's a difference between giving God the firstfruits of your day every morning and doing a quick Bible reading and prayer later in the afternoon. Giving God the firstfruits makes all the difference.

More Wisdom from the Upside-Down Kingdom
Matthew 5-7
The Sermon on the Mount

You have heard that it was said to the people long ago, "Do not murder, and anyone who murders will be subject to judgment." But I tell you that anyone who is angry with his brother will be subject to judgment. Again, anyone who says to his brother, "Raca," is answerable to the Sanhedrin. But anyone who says, "You fool!" will be in danger of the fire of hell....You have heard that it was said, "Do not commit adultery." But I tell you that anyone who looks at a woman lustfully has already committed adultery with her in his heart.

(Matthew 5:21-22, 27-28)

The spirit of the world says that only outward actions matter. God looks at the thoughts and intentions of our hearts.

Settle matters quickly with your adversary who is taking you to court. Do it while you are still with him on the way, or he may hand you over to the judge, and the judge may hand you over to the officer, and you may be thrown into prison. I tell you the truth, you will not get out until you have paid the last penny. (Matthew 5:25–26)

The spirit of the world is lawsuit-happy; it seeks its own profit and insists on its rights. But Jesus tells us to avoid contention and settle matters by making peace—or things could get out of hand. The Bible says, "If it is possible, as far as it depends on you, live at peace with everyone."

It has been said, "Anyone who divorces his wife must give her a certificate of divorce." But I tell you that anyone who divorces his wife, except for marital unfaithfulness, causes her to become an adulteress, and anyone who marries the divorced woman commits adultery. (Matthew 5:31–32)

The spirit of the world is casual about marriage vows. But God looks at marriage as a sacred and lifelong covenant between husband and wife.

You have heard that it was said, "Eye for eye, and tooth for tooth." But I tell you, Do not resist an evil person. If someone strikes you on the right cheek, turn to him the other also.

(Matthew 5:38–39)

The spirit of the world considers revenge an acceptable response to being wronged—almost an obligation. But God says that the only way to break the cycle of hatred and evil is to refuse to retaliate.

If someone wants to sue you and take your tunic, let him have your cloak as well. If someone forces you to go one mile, go with him two miles.

(Matthew 5:40–41)

The spirit of the world says we shouldn't let anyone take advantage of us. But God says we should surprise those who want to mistreat us by treating them with kindness and love—by showing them a better way.

You have heard that it was said, "Love your neighbor and hate your enemy." But I tell you: Love your enemies and pray for those who persecute you, that you may be sons of your Father in heaven. He causes his sun to rise on the evil and the good, and sends rain on the righteous and the unrighteous. If you love those who love you, what reward will you get? Are not even the tax collectors doing that? And if you greet only your brothers, what are you doing more than others? Do not even pagans do that? Be perfect, therefore, as your heavenly Father is perfect.

(Matthew 5:43–48)

The spirit of the world says, "Be good only to those who are good to you. It's okay to be bitter against your enemies." But God says, in effect, "Extend the same grace and forgiveness to your enemies that I show to everyone—to those who hate Me as well as those who love Me. Show that you are My children."

Be careful not to do your "acts of righteousness" before men, to be seen by them. If you do, you will have no reward from your Father in heaven. So when you give to the needy, do not announce it with trumpets, as the hypocrites do in the synagogues and on the streets, to be honored by men. I tell you the truth, they have received their reward in full. But when you give to the needy, do not let your left hand know what your right hand is doing, so that your giving may be in secret. Then your Father, who sees what is done in secret, will reward you. And when you pray, do not be like the hypocrites, for they love to pray standing in the synagogues and on the street corners to be seen by men. I tell you the truth, they have received their reward in full. But when you pray, go into your room, close the door and pray to your Father, who is unseen. Then your Father, who sees what is done in secret, will reward you....When you fast, do not look somber as the hypocrites do, for they disfigure their faces to show men they are fasting. I tell you the truth, they have received their reward in full. But when you fast, put oil on your head and wash your face, so that it will not be obvious to men that you are fasting, but only to your Father, who is unseen; and your Father, who sees what is done in secret, will reward you.

(Matthew 6:1-6, 16-18)

The spirit of the world says we should take credit or be acknowledged for every good thing we do to serve God and other people. But God says the motivation for our service shouldn't be honor; it should be love—love for God and love for others.

And when you pray, do not keep on babbling like pagans, for they think they will be heard because of their many words. Do not be like them, for your Father knows what you need before you ask him.

(Matthew 6:7-8)

The spirit of the world prefers religious formulas and rituals to genuine relationship with God because they eliminate the need for accountability. God desires a relationship of mutual trust and love with humanity that builds intimacy and promotes personal responsibility.

Do not store up for yourselves treasures on earth, where moth and rust destroy, and where thieves break in and steal. But store up for yourselves treasures in heaven, where moth and rust do not destroy, and where thieves do not break in and steal. For where your treasure is, there your heart will be also....No one can serve two masters. Either he will hate the one and love the other, or he will be devoted to the one and despise the other. You cannot serve both God and Money.   (Matthew 6:19-21, 24)

The spirit of the world says there is nothing beyond this life, so we should go after as much money, prestige, and influence as we can—while we can. God says that if we focus only on temporal things, we will lose out on eternal rewards. If we focus on eternal things, no one can ever take them away from us. It's impossible to be devoted to both God and worldly things.

Therefore I tell you, do not worry about your life, what you will eat or drink; or about your body, what you will wear. Is not life more important than food, and the body more important than clothes? Look at the birds of the air; they do not sow or reap or store away in barns, and yet your heavenly Father feeds them. Are you not much more valuable than they? Who of you by worrying can add a single hour to his life? And why do you worry about clothes? See how the lilies of the field grow. They do not labor or spin. Yet I tell you that not even Solomon in all his splendor was dressed like one of these. If that is how God clothes the grass of the field, which is here today and tomorrow is thrown into the fire, will he not much more clothe you, O you of little faith? So do not worry, saying, "What shall we eat?" or "What shall we drink?" or "What shall we wear?" For the pagans run after all these things, and your heavenly Father knows that you need them. But seek first his kingdom and his righteousness, and all these things will be given to you as well. Therefore do not worry about tomorrow, for tomorrow will worry about itself. Each day has enough trouble of its own.

(Matthew 6:25–34)

The spirit of the world is full of anxiety over not having enough or always wanting more.

God says that when we make His priorities our priorities, He will provide for everything we need so we can be free of worry and concentrate on eternal things.

Do not judge, or you too will be judged. For in the same way you judge others, you will be judged, and with the measure you use, it will be measured to you.

(Matthew 7:1–2)

The spirit of the world is very unforgiving. God says that, in the end, we will be treated in the way we have treated others.

Why do you look at the speck of sawdust in your brother's eye and pay no attention to the plank in your own eye? How can you say to your brother, "Let me take the speck out of your eye," when all the time there is a plank in your own eye? You hypocrite, first take the plank out of your own eye, and then you will see clearly to remove the speck from your brother's eye. (Matthew 7:3–5)

The spirit of the world is a critical spirit. It keeps a record of everyone else's faults but doesn't

*seem to recognize its own. God says we should
acknowledge and deal with our own faults before
trying to help others—or we will not only have
nothing to offer them, but we'll also look
ridiculous in the process.*

So in everything, do to others what you would have
them do to you, for this sums up the Law and the
Prophets. (Matthew 7:12)

*The spirit of the world says to look out for number
one. God says we should consider the interests and
welfare of others as if they are our own.*

You cannot love a
fellow-creature fully till
you love God.

—C. S. Lewis

Part III
Knowledge of the Glory

For God, who said, "Let light shine out of darkness," made his light shine in our hearts to give us the light of the knowledge of the glory of God in the face of Christ.

—2 Corinthians 4:6

When you're dull from all that glitters
When your thoughts have a hollow ring
When you can't escape from the feeling you're
getting it wrong...
All your foolproof plans seem foolish
All your status is status quo
All you really need to know is where you
belong.

Turn your eyes upon Jesus
Look full in his wonderful face
And the things of earth will grow strangely
dim
In the light of his glory and grace

"Where You Belong/Turn Your Eyes upon Jesus"
Shine: The Hits

*Whom have I in heaven but you? And
earth has nothing I desire besides you.
My flesh and my heart may fail, but
God is the strength of my heart and
my portion forever.*

—Psalm 73:25-26

There is only one happiness: to please Him.
—Thomas Merton

It was a rare moment. It was evening, and everything was quiet. Peter was sitting in his studio wondering about this sudden gift of solitude he had been given. Silence at that time of the day didn't happen very often. In the morning, there was always plenty of quiet, but the evening was a different story. There was usually some activity going on. But somehow, on this night, everything was still; the darkness outside seemed to cover all the noise and rush of the day. It was restful and comforting. While his wife, Summer, worked on a project upstairs, Peter sat in silent prayer and meditation before God for a full hour. He describes the experience in this way:

> The silence felt incredibly peaceful. There was no music playing, no television, no human voices. It was just God. And God is in the silence. I recently read a verse in 1 Kings that talks about God's gentle whisper. Elijah was waiting for the presence of the Lord, and there was a powerful wind and an incredible earthquake. Then the verse says, "After the earthquake came a fire, but the LORD was not in the fire. And after the fire came a gentle whisper." That's how God speaks to us. Just in that gentle whisper. But we have to be able to hear it.

The Bible talks about God walking in the Garden of Eden "in the cool of the day" in order to talk with Adam and Eve. Peter's experience was probably similar to what they must have experienced with God all the time before sin prevented them from having that shared life of intimacy with Him they had before the Fall.

Men and women were created to have communion with their Creator. This is why all of us need to be refreshed by the presence of our heavenly Father on a continual basis.

God speaks to us in a
gentle whisper. But we have
to be able to hear Him.

Without it, we lose connection with our Source of life. The daily wear and tear of living drains our spiritual strength and joy. We start struggling in our own strength, and then we have nothing left to give to others. We need time to reassess our priorities and learn to relate to the Father again.

One of the best gifts Christ gave us in bringing us the kingdom is the ability to have this intimate relationship with the Father. The apostle Paul wrote, "For God, who said, 'Let light shine out of darkness,' made his light shine in our hearts to give us the light of the knowledge of the glory of God in the face of Christ." Because Christ lives within us, He reveals the Father to us—illuminating our spiritual eyes to see and understand the "knowledge of the glory of God."

There is no better place to start seeking first the kingdom than by seeking the King Himself! Brother Lawrence said, "We can make our heart a chapel where we can go anytime to talk to God privately."

Some people call the special time they set apart to spend with God their "devotions," while others call it their "quiet time." Both terms are equally good, but it is a time of solitude, silence, and centering, where we set aside everything else and focus on God. That is when we really hear Him and come to know Him. Not in the winds and earthquakes of our never-ending activities and obligations.

It is vital for us to center on God because our spiritual lives can fall into a routine, just like the rest of our lives. For example, we might attend church every week, pay our tithes, say a quick prayer in the morning, and so on, but never really stop to hear what God is saying to us or express our love and gratitude to Him. We can become very comfortable in thinking that *doing* certain things is all that there is to our relationship with God. When this happens, we miss out on the joy of true communion with Him. Our relationship with God is always based on what Christ has done for us, rather than what we have "done" for God. When we are satisfied with doing things for God, rather than having fellowship with Him, this shows that we're still at the center of our lives, rather than the Lord. In the end, those works don't mean anything if we haven't done them for the sake of the kingdom.

In Isaiah, the Lord said, "These people come near to me with their mouth and honor me with their lips, but their hearts are far from me. Their worship of me is made up only of rules taught by men." God wants more than a religious routine from us. He desires our heartfelt love. As we seek first the kingdom, let it be our desire to show God that He is our first priority, and not let life crowd out the time we spend with Him, which we truly need.

> When we're satisfied with doing
> things for God rather than having
> fellowship with Him, this shows
> that we're still at the center of
> our lives, rather than the Lord.

Sometimes, when people make their first steps toward beginning or renewing intimacy with God, they struggle a little bit with how to go about it. That response is natural when dealing with anything that feels like new territory or a new experience. Any new relationship takes time to develop and grow. Each of us has a unique relationship with God because He has made us all individuals. You should give your relationship with God time to grow at its own pace and trust that God will meet you each step of the way. He desires this relationship even more than you do, and He is patiently waiting for you.

In this section of the book, we want to give you some guidelines for developing a meaningful relationship with God that have been helpful in our own spiritual lives.

"The Desire to Desire Him"

The best thing about living in the kingdom of God is that the King is also our Father! He is not just a distant ruler on a throne, but One with whom we can have close, daily contact. Because He is an all-powerful sovereign, He can meet our every need; and because He is our loving Father, He always has our best interests at heart. Jesus Himself taught us to begin our prayers by addressing God as Father. And that is the way we always need to come to Him.

For various reasons—busyness, fatigue, fear, guilt, laziness—many of us put off spending time with God. We seem to lack the desire to meet with Him. At those times, we need to remember God's promise to us:

I will give them an undivided heart and put a new spirit in them; I will remove from them their heart of stone and give them a heart of flesh. Then they will follow my decrees and be careful to keep my

laws. They will be my people, and I will be their God.

This idea is repeated in Philippians: "It is God who works in you to will and to act according to his good purpose." As someone said, "Even the desire to desire God comes from Him." In other words, everything we need—even the desire to love and fellowship with God—is something He must give us, for the sin nature within us resists this desire. However, the Spirit of Christ within us is much stronger than our sin nature, and as we surrender our need to God, He will change our hearts. Your prayer can be as simple as, "Father, help me to desire You." Keep praying this prayer with simple trust, and allow Him to kindle the love within your heart.

Grace and Acceptance

God desires us to love Him. This is more important to Him than all our efforts to please Him by doing or saying the right things. Many Christians have a real battle with trying to live up to the expectations they think God has for them. They're afraid to approach God because they remember all their failures and sins, and they don't think God will accept them. We must remember that all of us are imperfect. We all deal with problems, and we all make mistakes every day. What God looks at is our desire to love and serve Him.

One time, Jesus was invited to have dinner at a Pharisee's house. While He was there, a woman who had lived a sinful life came to visit Him because she had seen in Him the acceptance and forgiveness she desperately needed. She loved the Lord so much that she wept over Him and poured costly perfume on His feet. The Pharisee criticized her for being a sinner, but Jesus said, "Her many sins have been forgiven—*for she loved much.*" Then He said to her directly, "Your faith has saved you; go in peace." It was her love and simple faith that Jesus accepted.

The apostle Peter failed Jesus by denying Him three times on the night He was arrested. After Jesus was resurrected, He asked Peter three times, "Do you love me?" Peter answered, "Yes, Lord, you know that I love you." Jesus restored him and told him, "Feed my sheep." Later, Peter wrote in his first letter, "Above all, love each other deeply, because love covers over a multitude of sins." Perhaps Peter was remembering his own experience with Jesus' forgiveness when he wrote what he did. Although Peter had made a terrible mistake, he was restored because of Christ's sacrificial love for him and his devoted love for Christ.

No matter what we have done, God wants us to know that He is ready to accept us if we come to Him. Jeff has had his own struggle with feeling accepted by God, and we hope that reading what he has learned from his experience will help you understand how much God truly loves you.

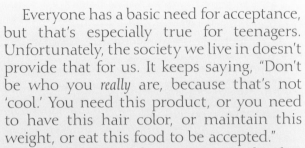

Everyone has a basic need for acceptance, but that's especially true for teenagers. Unfortunately, the society we live in doesn't provide that for us. It keeps saying, "Don't be who you *really* are, because that's not 'cool.' You need this product, or you need to have this hair color, or maintain this weight, or eat this food to be accepted."

I think a lot of times we apply that outlook to our relationship with God, thinking that if we don't do certain things, Jesus won't love us. But Jesus says, "Come to Me as you are. I accept you, just the way you are."

Really believing that is true for my own life is something I struggle with every day. Many times, I'll say to myself, "I am such a loser. I can't believe I did that," or "I can't believe I said that," or "I can't believe I committed that sin," and I'll let those negative feelings stand in the way of my relationship with God.

When I was growing up, I went to a Christian school that was extremely legalistic. I remember sitting through altar calls, bowing my head while the pastor spoke for half an hour, guilt-tripping everyone in the whole place. The Gospel was presented as a list of rules and regulations. That doesn't help when you put that on top of all the other things kids go through. It's hard when you're young, because everything is judged by certain measures. Your friends and peers judge you because they're your peer group, so there's a standard you have to live up to for them. You are judged by your grades and how well you do academically, so there's pressure in regard to that. Your parents have expectations of what they think you should be. Then there's your church, which has its own expectations of you.

So, in addition to all those pressures, I was dealing with what this school said I needed to do to be acceptable to God. In the process, I developed a habit of running away from God whenever I felt I'd done something wrong. So many times I try to "hide" from God. If I'm struggling with something, I'll let that totally keep me from Him, but in reality, He already knows everything about it!

No one ever really told me that God would accept me just the way I am, rules or legalities aside. And this is so important for *everyone* to know: God accepts you just the way you are. You don't have to change *anything* in order to come to Him, even if you already are a Christian. I hope that someone who really needs to hear this message will have a chance to hear it through this book.

God's grace is such an important thing. I wish I had understood it sooner. I wish somebody would have spent as much time telling me about grace as they spent telling me that my sideburns were too long or that I couldn't wear jeans to recess, or some crazy rule like that.

I didn't learn what grace really meant until recently, and it has changed my life dramatically. I think it scares a lot of people around me because, if anything, I may present myself as what a lot of people think of as less of a Christian, when really, I'm being more honest and transparent.

If you are having doubts about your acceptance with God, remember that when we confess our sins to Him, ask Him to cleanse us, and receive forgiveness through Christ, He promises not only to forgive our sins but also to forget them. Author Brennan Manning has said that he is a forgivable child of God—not failure-free, but forgivable. Grace means that we can come to God just as we are. He will welcome us enthusiastically and unconditionally. Then, in the context of His love, whatever needs to be changed in our lives will be transformed as we surrender to the life of Christ within us. Jesus illustrated God's unconditional love for us in the parable of the prodigal son:

> There was a man who had two sons. The younger one said to his father, "Father, give me my share of the estate." So he divided his property between them. Not long after that, the younger son got together all he had, set off for a distant country and there squandered his wealth in wild living. After he had spent everything, there was a severe famine in that whole country, and he began to be in need. So he went and hired himself out to a citizen of that country, who sent him to his fields to feed pigs. He longed to fill his stomach with the pods that the pigs were eating, but no one gave him anything. When he came to his senses, he said, "How many of my father's hired men have food to spare, and here I am starving to death! I will set out and go

back to my father and say to him: Father, I have sinned against heaven and against you. I am no longer worthy to be called your son; make me like one of your hired men." So he got up and went to his father. But while he was still a long way off, his father saw him and was filled with compassion for him; he ran to his son, threw his arms around him and kissed him. The son said to him, "Father, I have sinned against heaven and against you. I am no longer worthy to be called your son." But the

> The number one priority of the
> kingdom is to love God with
> all our heart, soul, mind,
> and strength—and this heartfelt
> devotion pleases God.

father said to his servants, "Quick! Bring the best robe and put it on him. Put a ring on his finger and sandals on his feet. Bring the fattened calf and kill it. Let's have a feast and celebrate. For this son of mine was dead and is alive again; he was lost and is found."

The beautiful thing about this story is that the prodigal was ten thousand steps away from his father, but when he made the decision to go home, in a sense, it was just one step back. This is a crucial truth for all of us to remember:

God is only ever one step away.

That step is going to Him in confession and repentance.

After we confess our sins, we aren't supposed to dwell on them. Instead, we're to focus on loving God with all our heart, soul, mind, and strength. That's the number one priority of the kingdom, and it's the heartfelt devotion that delights and pleases God.

Thomas Merton wrote a prayer that describes the confusion we often feel in life and how God accepts our devotion for Him, even when we understand very little about the rest of our lives:

> My Lord God, I have no idea where I am going. I do not see the road ahead of me. I cannot know for certain where it will end. Nor do I really know myself, and the fact that I think I am following you does not mean that I am actually doing so. But I believe the desire to please you does in fact please you. And I hope that I have that desire in all that I am doing. I hope that I will never do anything apart from that desire. And I know that if I do this, you will lead me by the right road, though I may know nothing about it. Therefore I will trust you always though I may seem to be lost and in the shadow of death. I will not fear, for you are ever with me, and you will never leave me to face my perils alone. Amen.

Trust

Understanding God's acceptance of us is essential to our relationship with Him, for without it, we won't feel that we can trust Him. Instead, we will feel like running away from Him all the time. Without trust, we can't have faith in God and His ways. Therefore, we won't make any progress in hearing and accepting His Word, which we must do to grow in Him. We also can't give Him the respect He deserves as our Creator and Father. When we fear God's punishment, rather than trust in His love and forgiveness, we won't respect Him—we'll resent Him because we'll feel that we can never please Him.

John Donne, the English poet and clergyman, came to this perspective when faced with the question of trusting God in the face of imminent death: "Trust represents the proper fear of the Lord." Trust is one of the greatest compliments we can give God because it shows we believe He is who He says He is. Our trust is based on what God says in His Word about who He is. As we hear and accept the Word, our trust will continually grow. Our trust honors God's nature and character and gives us a solid foundation for faith and prayer.

Desiring God, knowing that we are accepted by Him, and trusting Him are areas we must grow in as we seek the King of the kingdom. Through them, we can enter into a relationship with our heavenly Father in which He can teach us His ways and we can receive them in love and joy.

"Holy Habits"

- 🌞 Brother Lawrence called it "practicing the presence."

- 🌞 Jonathan Edwards defined it as "engagement of the heart" and "holy affection."

- 🌞 Francis de Sales used the term "spiritual agility."

- 🌞 John of the Cross called it "spiritual exercises."

- 🌞 Gregory of Nyssa said it was "becoming God's friend."

These are all descriptions of the ways in which we worship, reverence, love, learn from, surrender to, and serve God. Brother Lawrence wrote, "To be with Him, we must cultivate the holy habit of thinking of Him often." Mark Buchanan expands on this idea by saying, "Holy habits are...*the disciplines, the routines by which we stay alive and focused on Him.*"

We have found that the practice of a quiet time, devotions, or "holy habits" is somewhat subjective for each individual person, but the important thing is to make it a consistent part of our lives.

Some people have been taught to follow a certain mode of Bible study and prayer, but because it isn't working well for them, they are reluctant to do it. However, they are missing out on developing a close relationship with God. Sometimes this is because they are concentrating more on the method than on God Himself. If you are experiencing a similar situation, we encourage you to give yourself a little more freedom to try different methods that work for you and to trust God to guide you in this. Allow yourself time to grow in your devotional habits. Prayer and a love for God's Word are gifts from God, which He is pleased to give to you when you ask.

When I pray, I pray to God just like I'm talking to my mate. I start out by using the Lord's Prayer. I don't necessarily say the Lord's Prayer word for word, but I use that as my guide. Then I get to a point when I actually ask Him to reveal Himself to me, like when I was first saved. I'll say, "You know what, God? I've been a Christian for a long time, but I want You to be real to me. I want You to reveal Yourself to me." This is the incredible invitation that He yearns for us to ask Him. I never know what He's going to show me, but He does reveal Himself. This is part of seeking God first. I pray every day, "God, what will You have me to do? Reveal Yourself to me. With everyone I talk to today, guide my words so that maybe one phrase that I say will prick them in their hearts to bring them closer to You."

Solitude, Silence, and Centering

A relationship with God is like any other relationship: It doesn't happen automatically. We have to put our

 Shine

whole selves into it for it to be fulfilling and meaningful. The best place to start is with solitude, silence, and centering.

Elijah discovered that God is in the gentle whisper, and that is probably why most of us miss hearing Him—we're making too much noise! Solitude means finding a place that is away from the noise and busyness of everyday life so we can devote ourselves completely to our heavenly Father.

This is a time of "being still and knowing that He is God." It is physically and mentally becoming silent in preparation for hearing God speak to us through His Word and prayer. We do this by clearing out our internal distractions, such as jobs or household assignments, worry, or anger. Finding solitude is not the same thing as the world's method of stress relief by "clearing your mind and thinking of a happy place." If you are seeking God, and negative thoughts come at your mind, hand them over to the Father. Just keep handing them over to Him. As it says in the Psalms, "Cast your cares on the LORD and he will sustain you." When you keep casting your cares on the Lord, you will discover at some point that they are suddenly gone because you have handed them all over to Jesus.

Solitude is also a time of waiting. It is waiting on the Lord and learning to recognize the sound of the Shepherd's voice. Jesus said,

The man who enters by the gate is the shepherd of his sheep. The watchman opens the gate for him, and the sheep listen to his voice. He calls his own sheep by name and leads them out. When he has brought out all his own, he goes on ahead of them, and his sheep follow him because they know his voice.

This is a parable about Jesus Himself as the Good Shepherd. It is crucial that we learn to distinguish His voice

> We are all led by someone—either by ourselves, other people, or the Shepherd. If we have ears to hear, we will spend time learning to know the Shepherd's voice.

from our own ideas and the ideas of others that are contrary to the kingdom. The only way we can learn to know His voice is The only way we can learn to know His voice is by knowing what He has already said in His Word.

While we were on tour in New Zealand, we had the opportunity to visit the Agrodome, a big farm exhibition. Standing in a noisy crowd of people, we were amazed at how the sheepdog responded to his master's whistle. He knew the sound and obeyed the signals. If another man tried to communicate with him through different whistles,

it wouldn't work. The principle here is that we are all led by someone. We are led either by ourselves, other people, or the Shepherd. If we have ears to hear, we will spend time learning to know the sound of the Shepherd's voice.

When Samuel the prophet was a child, he was training to serve the Lord under Eli the priest. One night, Samuel heard a voice say, "Samuel!" Thinking it was Eli, Samuel jumped up and ran to him saying, "Here I am!" Eli said, "No, I didn't call you. Go back to bed!" This happened three times until Eli realized God was speaking to Samuel. He told him to lie down and when he heard God call his name, he was to answer, "Speak, LORD, for your servant is listening." Samuel did this, and then God spoke to him about what He was planning to do in the nation of Israel. From that time, Samuel knew the sound of the Lord's voice. Recognizing the Lord's voice takes some training. We have to be very familiar with the Bible, for whatever we truly receive from God will be in agreement with His Word.

Another benefit of being silent and centering on God is that it allows us to place our lives fully in His hands and trust Him to order them. Sometimes life is comparable to walking through a maze. We need to trust God to lead us along the right path. When we try to do things our own way, we run back and forth looking for an opening that will allow us to move forward, bumping into walls as we go. When we lose our way entirely, we start pacing in the labyrinthine cage we've created for ourselves.

But if we look up to God and ask Him to order our lives, if we ask Him for direction, then although we may not be able to see exactly where we're going, although we may not be able to see what's around the corner, we can trust Him to lead us in the right path. We might seem to be getting nowhere as we go through that maze. But we have only a limited perspective on things. God has complete perspective. Trusting Him to lead us is what it means to have faith in God and to seek Him first.

There are many spiritual rewards in the practice of solitude. The main thing is that, when we are quiet before the Lord, He knows He finally has our undivided attention. He can now encourage, strengthen, guide, and teach us as we seek His face.

"Ears to Hear"

The time we spend with God has more to do with our hearing God than anything else. When we hear and understand His Word—when we have "ears to hear," as Jesus said—that is when we will be able to pray effectively for His kingdom and will to be done on earth as it is in heaven.

The Bible says that the Spirit helps us to pray: "The Spirit helps us in our weakness. We do not know what we ought to pray for, but the Spirit himself intercedes for us with groans that words cannot express." We might be praying for a certain thing, but the Lord knows we need something else, and that's when the Spirit does His work of intercession for us. In the end, what we receive is according to the will of God. The Scriptures give us this assurance: "And he who searches our hearts knows the mind of the Spirit, because the Spirit intercedes for the saints in accordance with God's will.

The Scriptures also say, "If we ask anything according to his will, he hears us." There are certain prayers we can pray and *know* that God will always readily answer. These are prayers in which we ask Him to help us to become Christlike and to walk in His ways.

"Teach Me Your Ways"

First, we can constantly ask God to teach us His ways as we pray and read His Word. We can start by praying for wisdom, for if we understand the wisdom of the Lord and the necessity of abiding in Him, we're going to pray every day, read His Word every day, and treat other people with the love Christ has extended to us.

"Teach Me to Trust You"

We also can pray, "Lord, help me to trust in You and embrace You fully." Learning to trust is a process. We talked about trusting the character and nature of God as the basis for prayer and faith. Trust is a great thing because, in a sense, it's like being on a high wire without a net. It's total surrender of yourself. In other words, you have to give yourself to it fully in order to experience it.

"Help Me to Remember"

In addition, we can ask God to fill us with praise for Him. Each and every day, we need to remember what Christ has done for us because this will help us to have a thankful heart toward God. The psalmist said, "Enter his gates with thanksgiving and his courts with praise; give thanks to him and praise his name." We can be thankful for the day that the Lord has made; we can be thankful that He has given us another day to live. As G. K. Chesterton said, "Here dies another day during which I have had eyes, ears, hands, and the great world around me; and with tomorrow brings another. Why am I allowed two?"

We should begin each day with gratitude, as if it is a new start—because it is! God's mercies are new every morning.

"Help Me to Love Your Word and Understand Its Truths"

We need to ask God to help us love His Word and desire to read it. We also need to ask Him to reveal its truths to us. One of the problems in our generation is that we've become an illiterate people. Many of us—including many believers—do not know God's Word because we are not reading it, or, if we are, we don't have ears to hear what it is saying to us. But the Word is our spiritual lifeline, and we must read it to grow in the Lord and to know the voice of the Shepherd. Jesus said, "If you remain in me and my words remain in you, ask whatever you wish, and it will be given you. This is to my Father's glory, that you bear much fruit, showing yourselves to be my disciples."

The Bible says that the Word is "living and active." It is alive. If we develop a pattern of reading the Word daily because God has given us a love for it, then it won't be long before it will be impacting our lives or someone else's life with whom we come into contact. God said in Isaiah, "My word that goes out from my mouth...will not return to me empty, but will accomplish what I desire and achieve the purpose for which I sent it."

It's just a spirit thing

Some things in heaven cannot be explained.

Therefore, we should pray, "Lord, give me ears to hear Your Word." We've all probably had the experience of reading the Word with a deaf ear. We've read it but not really been aware of what the Spirit was trying to say to us. It comes down to being able to receive the Word, and that is something God does for us through His Holy Spirit. There is true joy in receiving revelation from God about His Word. There's massive joy when He reveals His ways to us by His Spirit. A. W. Tozer said the Holy Spirit takes the book of apologetics and transfers it to the human heart. That's really the key. The Holy Spirit takes the truths of theology and makes them alive *to* us and *within* us.

That is why we need to do some real digging into God's Word—as much as we would dig into the latest novel or Nintendo game. We can buy handbooks to help us understand the Bible better. Christians need to understand why they believe what they believe, or else their spiritual foundation will be weak. Perhaps you're at a place where you're not sure you even believe the Bible. You may just be going to church or youth group because you always have or because your family always has. Find out about Christ and Christianity for yourself. Do some research. If you ask God to reveal Himself to you, He will. This is something we have to trust. When we pray for revelation through the Scriptures, God answers us.

"Teach Me from the Wisdom You Have Given Your People"

Over the years, God has given many believers insights into His Word, which they have written down for the benefit of their own generations and later generations. Believers such as St. Augustine, St. Francis of Assisi, Charles Spurgeon, A. W. Tozer, C. S. Lewis, and Brennan Manning are among those whose challenging thoughts and inspiring ideas about God and His Word can greatly benefit our understanding of God and His ways. Sometimes they provide us with insights that we might never have understood on our own, so that our faith is truly strengthened after reading them.

Although their words can never be a substitute for the living and active Word, we can benefit spiritually from their experiences and the wisdom God has given them. When we read their books, we can pray, "Lord, help me to gain spiritual strength from what these believers have learned about You. Draw me closer to You through their words."

We can express our gratitude to God that we have these rich treasures of old and new Christian classics, whose truths people of any time and age can enjoy and benefit from. In the back of this book, we have included a section called "Books of Influence," which lists books that have been especially meaningful for us. We pray that you will take the time to read some of these gold mines of spiritual truth.

"Let Me Recognize Your Wonder"

Another thing we can pray for is the gift of wonder. The psalms often speak about the wonder of God's creation, so this is something that is very important to God. We take for granted so much of what God has given to us in His creation. But God wants us to recognize the beauty and glory of the world around us, whether it is in nature or in the things man has created out of the gifts God has given him—such as architecture and art. For example, wonder is seeing the vastness of the ocean and pondering the depth of the seas, thinking of the creatures God has created that live underneath its surface, all those strange and fascinating animals that we watch on "National Geographic."

Recognizing God's wonders means having ears to hear what the Spirit is revealing to us through creation. This not only means marveling over the beauty of the natural

> We take for granted God's creation.
> He wants us to recognize the beauty
> and glory of the world around us.

world but also learning the hidden lessons that God has built into nature. For example, when Jesus told us to "consider the ravens" and to "consider how the lilies grow," He was encouraging us to learn about God and His ways through the lovely and ordinary wonders around us. Solomon understood this when he pondered the actions of men and insects and said, "Go to the ant, you sluggard; consider its ways and be wise!"

Wonder is a youthful quality. In a sense, God is younger than we are. We're the ones who have finite bodies that were born at a certain time and will die at a certain time. God wasn't born and He isn't dying. He's eternal. When He says that we must become like little children to enter the kingdom of God, it is because He Himself has an everlasting youthful nature, and we are to reflect that, since our spirits will live eternally with Him.

We have a glimpse of our being made in His likeness when we see the excitement and joy on people's faces as they laugh out loud, when we see the rush of adrenaline in a crowd that is cheering a football player as he runs for a touchdown, when we see the look on children's faces as they watch fireworks bursting in the air, or when we see the spark of humor and life in the eyes of a ninety-five-year-old woman. We can see the glory of God in all these things because we're seeing the human spirit, made in His image. When you start thinking in this way, you will see the reflection of God's glory everywhere.

Wonder and glory are closely connected. G. K. Chesterton said something to the effect that, every day, when the sun comes up, God still gets excited about what He has created. Have you noticed that when you twirl a little kid around, and you've already whizzed him around twenty-five times, when you stop, he says, "Do it again, do it again!"? You think, *Oh, I've had enough!* but you whiz him around again, and he says, "Do it again, do it again!" God is like that, in a sense. He still takes pleasure in the sun coming up and going down, almost as if He's saying, "Do it again!" His pleasure in His creation is a youthful pleasure, and that is the attitude we should reflect, too.

To have the gift of wonder is also to marvel at God Himself. We can be full of wonder that God thought it was worth the risk of rejection when He gave mankind a free will, and worth the risk of total vulnerability when He sent His Son to die for the world. It is remarkable, when you think of it. But this is not the kind of wonder that makes us doubt God. Wonder is based on trust; it is based in the ultimate trust of God. Whatever scientists say about the origins of the earth, we trust that God is God, that He is the Creator, and that He sent His Son into the world

> God gets excited at His creation. He sees the sun coming up and going down, and it's as if He's saying, "Do it again!"

to die for us. When we trust in Him and His Word, we have massive freedom to marvel over all His ways, and to receive great pleasure and joy in doing so.

"Help Me to Live One Day at a Time"

There are a great many things we can learn from the Lord's Prayer, but one thing that is especially helpful for us in our day is understanding the phrase, "Give us today our daily bread." It seems as if we often focus much more on the future than on the day we're living in. Perhaps we've overemphasized the idea of "Where there is no vision, the people perish," so that we're constantly overlooking the meaning of today.

People think they need to know God's entire plan for their lives. But we forget the second half of the verse we just read. The entire verse reads, "Where there is no vision, the people perish: but he that keepeth the law, happy is he." This Scripture indicates that the vision that is being talked about is a revelation of God's law as a guide for our lives. It is talking about understanding and applying the ways of God more than having an idea of God's plans for our entire futures.

We often tell one another, "You need a vision for your life. What's the vision for your life?" The daily bread is what Christ taught us to pray for, but somehow we've turned it around so that we're focusing on things like where to go to college, what career to pursue, and so on. These things are important, but we can dwell on them while ignoring the people around us who are infinitely more valuable. Perhaps the vision doesn't always mean seeing down the road of our earthly lives. Maybe it means seeing eternal things. It's something to think about. Again, Christ instructed us to pray for our daily bread. He didn't say to ask what the future holds.

We need to keep everything on a daily basis. Remember that God's mercies are new every morning. Why are they new every morning? Because we *need them again* every morning! Every day, we can ask God to reveal to us how special that particular day is in His eyes. As it says in Psalms, "This is the day the LORD has made; let us rejoice and be glad in it."

Jesus Himself said, "Do not worry about tomorrow, for tomorrow will worry about itself. Each day has enough trouble of its own." Isn't that the truth! Therefore, we need to get back to the daily bread and the daily principle of living just a day at a time—because that is what Jesus did.

God's mercies are new every morning. Why? Because we need them fresh each and every morning.

"Make Me Aware of What You Are Doing in the World"

The Bible instructs us to "pray without ceasing." This is something we can practice daily, also. Part of praying without ceasing is responding to God as we become aware of Him and what He is doing in the world. There are many things happening all around us; the Spirit is working all the time in our lives and other people's lives, but we need to have ears to hear what the Spirit is saying. Again, we should pray, "Give me ears to hear," because we're often deaf to what God is doing. We miss things.

For example, we hear people on TV all the time expressing amazement over certain things they have experienced. An ambulance driver might say, "Yeah, well, the ambulance rolled over and we fell out and the patient still lived, so I guess the Good Lord must have had a hand in it." Of course He did! It might be just a strange experience to the ambulance crew, but if the driver were Billy Graham, he would have a different perspective on the incident. He would be more aware of what really happened.

There is another area of awareness that is very important. The more we press into God and the longer we do so, the easier it will be for us to discern that we have a spiritual enemy. As much as there is a true and living God, there is also a terrible, lying, conniving enemy. Satan will try to do his best to tear us away from our times of communion with the Lord. We need to be aware of this and guard against it.

Of course, when we are just starting to develop a quiet time, some of our reluctance to pray and read the Word is just our resistance to any type of discipline. We don't always wake up in the morning and say, "Oh, I just can't wait to spend time with the Lord." Sometimes we have to drag ourselves out of bed and make ourselves do it, but in the end, we'll always be glad we did.

Our reluctance to spend time with God will change as we grow closer and closer to Him through our "holy habits." When we truly have an encounter with the living God, we are never the same. We *desire* to spend time with Him. For instance, when we truly fall in love with someone, we experience a natural draw to that person. There's also a discipline that comes with it as well, but it is more of a natural discipline. There are certain things in regard to the relationship that we feel, "I have to do this because this relationship is so important to me that I want to maintain it." It isn't a discipline that is a terrible burden. It's just something that has to be done in order for us to have a successful relationship. The same is true of our relationship with the Lord. We become aware of what elements are essential to building and maintaining communion with Him.

Having ears to hear is such an essential spiritual skill that we now want to explore two more areas where we need to exercise it in our lives: Sabbath Rest and Defining Moments.

Sabbath Rest

Awareness is all in how we walk. If we "keep in step with the Spirit," we will remain in the presence of God. However, if we try to rush ahead of God in our busyness, we will miss out on our relationship with Him, as well as all the good things He is doing in the world that we need to be aware of. Busyness is a major danger and temptation for all of us because in our society we're experiencing an attack on our time.

Technology is becoming intrusive in our lives, as we talked about in the first section of this book. Cell phones, the Internet, E-mail, and faxes keep us wired up and going constantly. Although we enjoy their convenience and the way they help us keep in touch with other people, if we let them bring constant noise and distractions into our lives, we won't have ears to hear the Lord. These things can keep us from having the solitude and silence we need in order to center on God. They also leave us overtired and irritable, because our busyness prevents us from getting the rest we need. It is difficult for the light of Christ to shine through us when we're disagreeable from a lack of rest.

The challenge for us is not to let technology eat away at the time we need to be spending with God and our families, time we need to build relationships and encourage one another in the Lord.

What would the effect on your family be if you followed certain guidelines to keep the busyness of the world from overpowering your life? For example, what if you were to make no business calls after six o'clock? What if you decided, "Work is over. I am going to spend time with my family and take care of family needs. The cell phone is going to be shut off because, otherwise, I'm going to be interrupted constantly"? Maybe we need the courage to take steps like this, as many of us work ourselves half to death.

Our Creator has given us certain principles for living for a reason. The principle of Sabbath rest is one of them. God commanded the Israelites to take a day of rest from their work and to honor Him. He also gave similar guidelines for the land. Every seven years, the land was not to be farmed, but was to be allowed to "rest." This is because the soil is depleted of nutrients each year by the crops, and it needs to be renewed. In a similar way, God has designed us to need rest, to need some times of quiet and solitude, so that we can be renewed in body, soul, and spirit. We aren't meant to deal with a lot of stress.

We can get really busy, can't we? We get far too busy in life. I've had to cut back on a lot of things that I've been involved in and just spend more time at home, more time in the garden even, more time just outside and walking around my neighborhood and bumping into people and talking to them. When my neighbor from down the street wants to stop and talk to me, I need to have the time to talk to him because there's nothing more important than for me to communicate and connect with another human being. That's so important. I've noticed in the last couple of years that I've had to reassess my priorities regarding what I'm spending my time on—what I'm spending my time thinking about and who I'm spending my time with. I've had to reshuffle, and it's been a really good and purifying time of simplifying and getting everything in perspective.

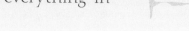

I haven't had a cell phone for several years because I was getting more calls on my cell phone than the White House switchboard. I occasionally experienced some withdrawal, but I have good friends, and I belong to cell phones anonymous (just kidding).

I don't think there's anything wrong with cell phones in themselves. They're really convenient. But for me, in my life, having a cell phone wasn't a great thing because I was abusing it. Getting rid of my cell phone was a tough thing for me to do, but I just did it unto the Lord, and it's been a really good thing for me and for my family. You see guys out at restaurants at 8:30 at night with their wives and families, talking business on their cell phones. Five years ago, people wouldn't be conducting business at the dinner table like that. (con't)

We're not built that way. Because of the Fall, many things have come into play that we weren't originally built to deal with.

In our culture, it would be a *very* powerful witness to the world if believers became a people who were *rested*, who understood the concept of Sabbath rest. The contrast would be striking.

Everyone has his own convictions regarding observing the Sabbath. For example, some people will shop on Sunday; others won't. Issues such as those aren't as much

(con't)

It's not so much a knock on cell phones, but it's the principle of shutting down, the principle of Sabbath rest for the land, like the Bible talks about in Leviticus. It's the idea of letting the land rest for a year, so that others have the opportunity to come and glean something from it.

But if I see someone with a cell phone, I don't criticize him; rather, I feel, "But for the grace of God, there go I." If it wasn't for the grace, I'd have one right now. And this is just what I have decided for my own life. I'm not saying it's for everybody. But it's been an excellent decision for me.

the point as much as the *principle* of rest and the fact that Christians, as much as the world—or maybe more so—don't make a habit of taking days or periods of much-needed rest. This is a truly serious issue that hinders us from being the light of the world.

Peter did an experiment to see what would happen if he applied the principle of Sabbath rest:

A couple of years ago, I was burning out big time, where I'd work seven days a week on a record, in the middle of a project, thinking that I would be getting it done quicker, but I found out that was a lie. One day, I thought, *I'm going to experiment with this.* So I just started taking one day a week off. All of a sudden, I was twice as productive, I thought more clearly, I was rested, I was more tolerable to be around, and the world felt like a better place. Now, one or two days a week, I just shut everything down, and I've really felt rested and empowered by that.

As we ask God to teach us His ways and give us ears to hear in regard to this area of Sabbath rest, we should remember that Jesus made these significant statements concerning it: "The Sabbath was made for man, not man for the Sabbath. So the Son of Man is Lord even of the Sabbath." The Sabbath was given for our benefit, to prevent us from overextending ourselves and harming ourselves physically, emotionally, or spiritually. Since Christ is Lord of the Sabbath, and we are to yield to His life within us so that we can be the light of the world, each of us should ask Him how He would like us to live and in what ways we need to incorporate Sabbath rest into our lives.

Defining Moments

Since understanding and being aware of the way God works in our lives is so important, we now want to talk about reasons we may miss what He is trying to say to us.

Our friend and Bible study teacher, Pastor Ray McCollum, gave a talk entitled, "Defining Moments," which highlighted these reasons. This section is a summary of the major points he brought out in that study.

In its November 12, 2001, issue, *Christianity Today* magazine ran a cover story of President Bush with the title, "Bush's Defining Moment." The story was about how the events of September 11 transformed his whole presidency. Less than a year before, he had been barely elected to office, and he had the challenge of trying to lead a country that was divided right down the middle. But the terrorist attack on America transformed President Bush so much that everybody, even his enemies, noticed the difference it made. He moved forward with purpose and focus, and the whole country united behind him. One of Bush's aides, Timothy Goeglein, said that the 9-11 tragedy was "absolutely a spiritually defining moment for the country and its leader."

Defining moments are those identifying points in time that change the course of our lives forever. They are God's encouragements along the road of life. We must learn to recognize and embrace them because their purpose is to shape both our relationship with God and our future.

An excellent example of someone who had a defining moment is Jacob. Here is the background of his story: He was the second-born of twins. As the twins were being delivered, Jacob had his hand on his brother's heel, as if to trip him up so that he could get ahead of him. This was the way he was for the entire first half of his life. He would do anything to get the blessing. He didn't care who he had to trip up to do it. He persuaded his brother, Esau, to trade his birthright for a bowl of stew and then deceived his father in order to steal the blessing that his brother was supposed to receive. After he did that, he had to run away to escape Esau's wrath.

Twenty years later, we find him journeying home to face the music. He knows he will meet up with his brother the next day. It's a crisis in his life, but in that time of crisis, he will have a defining moment. Defining moments have often been known to happen during crises. Let's pick up the story at that point:

> Jacob was left alone, and a man wrestled with him till daybreak. When the man saw that he could not overpower him, he touched the socket of Jacob's hip so that his hip was wrenched as he wrestled with the man. Then the man said, "Let me go, for it is daybreak." But Jacob replied, "I will not let you go unless you bless me." The man asked him, "What is your name?" "Jacob," he answered.

The defining moment comes in the next verse:

> Then the man said, "Your name will no longer be Jacob, but Israel, because you have struggled with God and with men and have overcome."

God actually changed his name. Then Jacob said,

"Please tell me your name." But he replied, "Why do you ask my name?" Then he blessed him there. So Jacob called the place Peniel, saying, "It is because I saw God face to face, and yet my life was spared." The sun rose above him as he passed Peniel, and he was limping because of his hip.

Here we have a man who has been a Jacob all his life, but now God says in this moment of crisis, in effect, "I'm going to redefine you." He is never the same after this. He even walks differently. This is the first time we read the name *Israel* in the Bible. It is given to a man who is going to become the father of a whole nation. In *redefining* Jacob, God also *defined* the nation that would come out of him.

As we grow in our relationship with God and learn to understand and accept His ways, He redefines us. He does this by bringing us through certain experiences, or bringing certain people into our lives, to change us, so that we will never be the same. Learning how to recognize and embrace these moments requires ears to hear what God is saying to us during these times. There are five main reasons why we may miss defining moments from God.

A Defining Moment May Not Seem Like a Positive Experience

The first reason we may miss a defining moment is that it does not always seem like a positive experience at the time. Jacob's situation was not initially a pleasant one. It was night. He was alone. He was wrestling with someone whom he thought was a man, but turned out to be God! Wrestling with God was a struggle for Jacob, but out of that encounter came a significant redefinition not only of his name, but of his entire life. In the end, it was a very good moment.

Joseph also began with a bad experience. The moment that started him on the road to his destiny was when he was betrayed and sold into slavery by his own brothers. How do you suppose he felt? He was probably fighting a lot of bitterness. Yet this was God's moment, which took him in a whole new direction that eventually led to his being second-in-command to Pharaoh in Egypt. This position enabled him to provide for his family so they didn't starve during the great famine. When Joseph was reunited with his brothers, he said, "You intended to harm me, but God intended it for good to accomplish what is now being done, the saving of many lives." The older we get, the more we can look back and see how God really does make even the bad things work together for our good.

A Defining Moment May Not Be What We Expect

Second, sometimes we can miss a defining moment because it comes in a form we don't expect.

There are many examples in the Bible where people missed their moment, or almost missed it, because they didn't get what they expected. John the Baptist came out of the wilderness eating bugs, wearing camel's hair, and preaching a strange message. He wasn't what the religious leaders expected.

The greatest example of this point is Jesus Christ Himself. The whole nation of Israel was expecting the Lion of Judah, and they got the Lamb of God. Their frustration with Jesus was not so much that He healed the sick or ministered to people who were hurting, but that He wouldn't drive the Romans out and reestablish the kingdom of David in their time. Because He wasn't what they expected, many missed Him altogether.

A Defining Moment May Not Be Sudden

Third, a defining moment may not happen suddenly. It may seem as if Jacob's defining moment happened in a sudden way, but he had been preparing for it for twenty years. During that time, God had been working on Jacob's character. He was getting Jacob ready to go back home, getting him ready to have his defining moment.

Let's look at the example of David. He didn't suddenly become king. He was anointed king three times. It took a number of years before he was truly ruling the kingdom of Israel. Moses was called at age forty. Abraham had his child of promise when he was one hundred and Sarah was ninety years old. We can go through a series of events, or a season of time, that is a defining moment. It doesn't have to be something that happens in an instant. This is why perspective is so important. We can't understand certain things when they are happening, but we can look back and see the pattern of God in our lives. It is important to trust God in all situations because we don't know what He might be working out in our lives that we will discover later.

Defining Moments Are Not Always Spectacular

Fourth, a defining moment isn't always a spectacular event. The Old Testament tells the story of Naaman, who was the commander of an army and a leper. When he heard that Elisha the prophet might be able to help him, he went to visit him. Elisha heard that he was coming to be healed and he sent his servant out to tell him to dip seven times in the muddy Jordan River, and he would be healed. Naaman was offended at this advice. He thought this man of God would come out and make a spectacular show while healing him. Some people want God to appear to them in person or show some miraculous sign when He is about to do something in their lives. But most of the defining moments in our lives won't *seem* very spectacular. Most of them will happen in our everyday lives.

Defining Moments Won't Usually Happen to Us Alone

Defining moments almost always involve other people. Sometimes the relational aspect will be other people helping to make the defining moment happen in your life. But in some way or another, your defining moment will eventually affect other people.

Again, this is what happened to Jacob. He came to his moment and had an experience with God, and God redefined him by changing his name. In this act, God not only was renaming Jacob, but He also was renaming all of Jacob's descendants. Everything that happened to Jacob in that moment by extension affected the nation of Israel.

The last thing we read about Jacob in the Bible is in Hebrews 11, where he is listed in the faith hall of fame. It says, "By faith Jacob, when he was dying, blessed each of Joseph's sons, and worshiped as he leaned on the top of his staff." What does this say about him? It tells us that Jacob's defining moment changed the way he walked before God. It changed the way he worshipped for the rest of his life.

There is a saying that goes, "I wouldn't walk with a man who doesn't have a limp." It is referring to a man who has not been through the dealings of God, a man who has not been redefined by God. When Jacob worshipped leaning on his staff, that was a prophetic picture of what real worship is. Only when you know that it is God who is holding you up in all things can you really worship Him. When someone has never had such a defining moment, his worship goes only so deep.

Let's look now at how God gives us these defining moments in our lives and at how to recognize and embrace them.

To define someone is a function of authority and responsibility. Since God is the ultimate authority, He is the only One who has the absolute right to define His creation. That includes us. Our primary way of knowing who we are is through the Word of God, which tells us the purpose for which God made us.

God has defined what it takes to be His child. He has defined what it takes to be a disciple. When we yield our lives to Christ, it is no longer about us making up our own minds about who we are, but about our finding out who God says we are. The greatest defining moment we ever have is when we meet Christ and are called God's children.

When Jacob was wrestling with God, he asked God to bless him. God responded by asking him his name. It wasn't that God didn't know Jacob's name, but that He wanted Jacob to learn something significant. When Jacob spoke his own name, which means "supplanter," it was his way of owning up to his personal character defects. Because he recognized he was with God, he was asking God to redefine him, to give him a different life from the one he had led up to that point.

Here is the key: Every time God reveals Himself to you so that you really see Him in a fresh way, He is going to speak something to you that will redefine you for life. For example, when Peter was able to recognize who Jesus really was, when he was able to define Jesus, he said, "You are the Christ, the Son of the living God." Jesus' response was to define Peter in a new way: "I tell you that you are Peter, and on this rock I will build my church, and the gates of Hades will not overcome it." It was a beautiful, mutual revelation, and God wants to do the same in our relationship with Him.

> Every time God reveals Himself
> to you so that you see Him in
> a fresh way, He is going to
> speak something to you that will
> redefine your life.

The Light of His Glory

As we learn to have ears to hear, and as we discover how to commune with our heavenly Father, our encounters with Him on a daily basis will be times of real transformation. He will continually conform us to the image of Christ by redefining who we are, changing us from people who are controlled mainly by our sinful nature, to people who are controlled by the Spirit of Christ. That is when the light of His glory will truly be seen in us so that it can transform the world around us.

Until you are surrendered you are a "self-ian"; when you are surrendered you are a "Christ-ian," a Christian.

—E. Stanley Jones

Part IV

The Fruit of the Light

The fruit of the light consists in all goodness, righteousness and truth.

—Ephesians 5:9

Why you holdin' grudges in old jars?
Why you wanna show off all your scars?
What's it gonna take to lay a few burdens
down?
It's a beautiful sound

When they all fall
Like a million raindrops
Falling from a blue sky
Kissing your cares goodbye
They all fall
Like a million pieces
A ticker tape parade high
And now you're free to fly

"Million Pieces"
Thrive

For this very reason, make every effort
to add to your faith goodness; and to
goodness, knowledge; and to knowledge, self-
control; and to self-control, perseverance;
and to perseverance, godliness; and to
godliness, brotherly kindness; and to
brotherly kindness, love. For if you possess
these qualities in increasing measure, they
will keep you from being ineffective and
unproductive in your knowledge of our Lord
Jesus Christ.

—2 Peter 1:5–8

The self is not canceled when surrendered. It is heightened. A plus is added to all we do and say and are, a divine plus.
—E. Stanley Jones

When children plant seeds in the ground, they often expect to see a full-grown flower or vegetable the very next day. They don't understand that seeds have to go through a process of growth in order to mature and bear fruit. As children of God, many of us think in a similar way; we expect our spiritual growth to happen overnight. We look for perfection in ourselves, and we often expect it of other believers, even when they are very new Christians.

God is still at work within all of us. Although He does make immediate changes in our lives when we are born again, that is just the beginning of a lifelong maturing process as He develops us into the image of His Son.

Spiritual Seasons

The spiritual growth that we experience occurs in "seasons." We're all in different seasons in our spiritual lives as well as our physical lives. Charles Swindoll wrote, "Seasons are designed to deepen us, to instruct us in the wisdom and ways of our God."

Remember that repentance brings "times of refreshing" as we change our hearts and minds and follow the ways of Christ. We will experience many of these times of repentance and refreshing as God takes us through various seasons of growth. Our heavenly Father calls us to an ever deepening walk with Him in which we "fix our eyes on Jesus, the author and perfecter of our faith." Our journey is to be, as Eugene Peterson says, "a long obedience in the same direction." As we travel, we will have some ups and downs. Duncan describes how this process has worked in his own life and in all our lives:

Having been a Christian for approximately twenty years now, looking back, I've noticed different seasons to the life of faith. We've also had many seasons corporately within the band, and out of these seasons, more than just the music, a real bond has developed between us. I've really grown to admire them as brothers, seeing the growth in their personal faith with the Lord. Hopefully, each of them can say the same thing about me. I know that I'm not the man I was ten years ago, thank God. We need to progress, to go on, to develop, and grow. If we don't, we're almost going backward, aren't we?

We've seen how God moves in our lives personally and corporately. We are told in 2 Peter that becoming a mature believer means adding more and more of the characteristics of Christ to the foundation of our faith. As we go through spiritual seasons, we may at times feel stretched to the limit, but God knows how much we can bear. He is our Father, and He won't allow us to become overwhelmed. He will always sustain us in His love.

Spiritual growth has seasons.
We must remember that winter
is a season as much as spring.

The Way of Surrender

It is God's goal to help us become mature Christians in whom the Spirit of Christ is clearly manifested. Our heavenly Father nurtures us during our daily times of communion with Him. As we pray, "Teach me Your way," the way He will show us is the way of surrender. This is because the essence of the character of Christ is total submission to the Father. He humbled Himself, not only by becoming a man but also by becoming the *Servant* of men. Jesus said, "The Son of Man did not come to be served, but to serve, and to give his life as a ransom for many."

Again, hearing and accepting the Gospel of the kingdom means hearing and accepting a life of surrender that will allow the nature of Christ to be seen in our lives "in increasing measure"—surrendering not to please men or yourself but in reverence, as a sacrifice to Christ. The way of surrender is the key to reaping a fruitful harvest for the kingdom—a bounty of love, grace, forgiveness, joy, truth, righteousness, and peace. This bounty is the fruit of the light in us, through which others will be able to "taste and see that the LORD is good."

> As we pray, "Teach me Your
> way," the way He will show us
> is the way of surrender.

Two Ways of Transformation

"Teach me Your way" is like this heartfelt prayer of David's:

Search me, O God, and know my heart; test me and know my anxious thoughts. See if there is any offensive way in me, and lead me in the way everlasting.

In answer to this prayer, God, who knows our hearts, will start to show us areas in our lives that we need to surrender to Him so they can be transformed. He does this in two ways. First, the Holy Spirit will bring conviction in our own hearts. Second, God may use others in the body of Christ to show us ways in which we need to grow in Him. This is especially true if we are connected to a vital and joyful Christian community that understands transformation through grace. When God does use other believers to help us grow, He will confirm in our own hearts what He is trying to teach us.

God uses both of these methods because, in the Christian life, there are certain things a believer must do for himself, while there are other things he can do only in community with other believers. As spiritual beings, each of us is personally responsible before God for the way we

---

We are meant to live in covenant with
our brothers and sisters in Christ.
There are no "Lone Ranger" Christians.

---

live our lives. For example, others can't repent for us or obey God for us. However, we are also meant to live in covenant with our brothers and sisters in Christ. There are no "Lone Ranger" Christians. Teaching, discipleship, fellowship, worship, and service are meant to be shared activities in the community of God.

The apostle Paul gave us valuable insight into this truth when he wrote:

Brothers, if someone is caught in a sin, you who are spiritual should restore him gently. But watch

yourself, or you also may be tempted. Carry each other's burdens, and in this way you will fulfill the law of Christ. If anyone thinks he is something when he is nothing, he deceives himself. Each one should test his own actions. Then he can take pride in himself, without comparing himself to somebody else, for each one should carry his own load.

"Each one should carry his own load," but we are also to "carry each other's burdens." Personal responsibility and a loving and nurturing community are both essential for growing in the grace and knowledge of Christ.

Losing Ourselves

Jesus said, "If anyone would come after me, he must deny himself and take up his cross and follow me. For whoever wants to save his life will lose it, but whoever loses his life for me will save it." To experience the abundant life, we have to die to ourselves. Jesus explained this mystery of dying in order to live by saying,

Unless a kernel of wheat falls to the ground and dies, it remains only a single seed. But if it dies, it produces many seeds. The man who loves his life will lose it, while the man who hates his life in this world will keep it for eternal life. Whoever serves me must follow me; and where I am, my servant also will be. My Father will honor the one who serves me.

If a kernel of wheat is kept safely protected in a jar on a shelf, it doesn't really do anyone any good. To produce fruit that can nourish life in others, the kernel has to be buried in the ground. Its "death" will result in life. In the same way, when we die to our selfish desires, we allow Christ's life to take root in our hearts.

We start this process of dying to ourselves by being completely honest with God about who we are and what we have done. David said, "Surely you desire truth in the inner parts; you teach me wisdom in the inmost place."

We start the process of dying to ourselves by being completely honest with God about who we are and what we have done.

Truth is part of holiness. David was a man who sinned greatly by committing adultery and killing a man. Yet he was also called a man after God's own heart. What God seemed to love about him was that he was quick to repent when he was confronted with his sin. He was truthful to God about it, rather than denying it.

Honesty with God is a crucial step to take, for if we aren't being honest with God, then we're not being honest with ourselves. When we're not honest with ourselves, it's difficult to be honest with other people. It's also likely that we will not have an honest opinion of *them*. Instead, we will have a judgmental opinion. Most of us recognize that we are quick to criticize others who have the same faults as we do.

How do we overcome the dilemma of needing to be honest with God but not wanting to admit our sin to Him? It is grace that gives us the freedom to be truthful and real. Paul wrote, "Therefore, there is now no condemnation for those who are in Christ Jesus, because through Christ Jesus the law of the Spirit of life set me free from the law of sin and death." When we are motivated by fear of condemnation, we will be defensive. But when we understand His unconditional love for us, we can be open about our faults without feeling crushed by them. Confession to God leads to repentance, restoration, and refreshing—not condemnation.

Too often we view death to self from a negative perspective. Although it is true that the act of losing ourselves requires giving up certain things, we need to view it as the natural spiritual process that it is. As we become more like Christ, we become less. In essence, we begin to die. As we are continually conformed into what the Lord wants us to be, His nature in us increases while our sin nature decreases.

Dying to self is not something that we're necessarily conscious of. We don't think to ourselves, "I'm dying to myself now." But to a certain extent, we know that we are. Dying to self involves giving up our way of doing things, not making this sacrifice for attention or to win the approval of others, but as unto the Lord, as a sacrifice unto Him. Christ gave up His right to glory in order to become the Servant of men, and He is our Example. So much of being a follower of His means giving up our way of doing things and gaining the attitude of Christ. The more we start filling ourselves with Christ, with what He is about and what He wants, and the more we truly become sensitive to what the Holy Spirit is teaching us about ourselves, the less we become.

> Being Christ's followers means
> giving up our way of doing things
> and gaining the attitude of Christ.

The Eye of the Needle

Jesus used another example to describe what it means to die to self in order to live in "newness of life." He said, "It is easier for a camel to go through the eye of a needle than for a rich man to enter the kingdom of God." Can you picture a camel trying to squeeze through the small opening in a needle? The idea seems ridiculous. It leaves us with a clear realization: It's impossible!

Jesus was saying that people's possessions can be so valuable to them that they've lost eternal perspective and true reality. They would rather hold on to their wealth than abandon it to follow Him—even at the cost of eternal life. But as we said earlier, it's not just the wealthy who have trouble entering the kingdom of God. All of us struggle to some extent with wanting our own way. We think we can come up with a plan to push that camel through. But our efforts at saving ourselves are hopeless. We finally ask the same question the disciples asked: "Who then can be saved?" And we hear Jesus' grace-filled response, "With man this is impossible, but with God all things are possible."

This is the key: It can be done only through God, not through our own efforts. Knowing this truth enables us to stop struggling in our own strength in trying to die to ourselves. We can rest in the fact that when we surrender to Christ, He will take us through the eye of the needle.

When we surrender to Christ, He will take us through the eye of the needle.

It's a mystery, isn't it, to understand what it means to serve in an upside-down kingdom? This concept of going through the eye of the needle will make sense to us only when we experience it firsthand by leaving ourselves behind and going through it in Christ.

Although His grace takes us through the eye of the needle, we first have to be willing to leave our carnal selves behind. Even after we have become Christians, we still have to struggle with our tendency toward self-preservation and self-promotion. The people who make a real difference in this world are the ones who have lost themselves, who have moved through the eye of the needle and left themselves behind.

"As unto the Lord"

What it really means to lose oneself for the sake of Christ began to come clear to Peter when God showed him how he was to apply it in his relationship with his wife:

> I always struggled with the Scripture that said, "Husbands, love your wives, just as Christ loved the church," because I'm not Christ, so what did that mean? This is what God revealed to me. I'm not saying this is *the* way for everyone, but this is what He revealed to me: Every time I feel that I have to make a compromise, that is, if I have to lose myself over a certain issue, what He taught me was, "Don't do it to have a great marriage. Don't do it to make your wife happy. Do it as a sacrifice *as unto Me.*" And that's a secret that broke open my married life. I've been married for eleven years now, and it's made it all new again. It's made it the best that it's ever been.

> Husbands can hold on to this idea of, "Hey, I go out and earn a good living, so I deserve my space." The Lord has helped me to surrender that barrier

that I used to put up between us. For the last couple of years, my wife has often been on the road with us. It's been excellent because, before, I needed my space. But God has changed that, and my space is not there anymore. It has slowly dissipated, and that's been excellent. There's major joy in that.

The way we lose ourselves or surrender ourselves is to do everything "as unto the Lord." Our attitude is not, "I'm going to surrender because I'm going to get in deep trouble if I don't," or "She's going to be mad at me and I don't want to deal with that." It's not like that. The whole focus of service is doing it as if we were doing it for the Lord.

A surrendered heart is not defensive.
When your barriers are torn down,
God can give you true communication
with others.

We might have to stop and say, "Okay, Lord, this is a tough one. I need Your help to let go of selfishness and to do this as unto You," but God always answers that prayer. He will come through with grace and peace and give us the ability to follow through.

Often, God will teach us new lessons as we make the effort to put others first. For instance, suppose you call out to your wife, "I'm going down to Home Depot," and she calls back, "What are you going there for?" That could trigger a reaction in you, such as "What do you care where I'm going? I'm just going to Home Depot. What's your problem?" But a surrendered heart is not defensive, and when those self-imposed barriers are torn down, God can reveal what the other person is really saying. You can understand that your wife just wants to be involved with what you are doing. While you're thinking, "I'm going to Home Depot to buy a hammer," she sees it as an opportunity to spend time together. Maybe she wants to talk things over with you—like the paint she saw for the back bedroom or some new light fixtures for the porch.

> Not all service is servanthood. Do we sincerely want to serve God and reach out to His children?

Another lesson about surrender is that not all service is real servanthood. It's easy to serve the people we want to serve and ignore the ones who require us to really give of ourselves. In fact, it's often easier for us to serve complete strangers than it is to serve our own families and friends. For example, if you see a poor man on the street and he asks you for money, it's quite easy to give it. You can throw some change his way and begin to think quite highly of yourself, so that you're serving your ego rather than serving "as unto the Lord." When we do something like this, we miss the heart of what it means to lose ourselves for Christ's sake.

This doesn't mean that we won't have a good feeling when we do something to help someone else. The question is, What was our motivation for what we did? Did we do it to impress someone else? Did we do it to make up for a selfish act we committed yesterday? Or did we do it because we sincerely want to serve God and reach out to His children, because we believe Jesus when He taught,

> "I was hungry and you gave me something to eat, I was thirsty and you gave me something to drink, I was a stranger and you invited me in, I needed clothes and you clothed me, I was sick and you looked after me, I was in prison and you came to visit me." Then the righteous will answer him, "Lord, when did we see you hungry and feed you, or thirsty and give you something to drink? When did we see you a stranger and invite you in, or needing clothes and clothe you? When did we see you sick or in prison and go to visit you?" The King will reply, "I tell you the truth, whatever you did for one of the least of these brothers of mine, you did for me."

Serving with the right motivation is essential. There is a big difference between serving others because we feel sorry for them and serving them out of compassion. Sometimes feeling sorry for people means that you want to help them only because they're making you feel bad, and you don't like feeling that way, rather than being genuinely concerned for them.

Ultimately, servanthood starts in the home. That's where we really learn what it means to deny self. Peter describes how he came to understand this truth:

> Marriage is a good place for learning to die to yourself. It's a great thing. I say that with joy. I'd be in such a bad place if I wasn't married.

> I understood the principle of losing yourself, and I practiced it with the people it was easiest to practice it with, until I finally realized, "I've been thinking I'm something great because I'm doing this person a favor." It has to come down to being able to serve anyone, not just those we want to serve.

> My defining moment in understanding all this came when my relationship with my wife wasn't working; it was going downhill. I was thinking I was being the servant by being out there "serving" others, when I was neglecting my wife, the person I should be serving the most.

This brings out another important point. If our serving one person causes us to hurt someone else, we'd better take a closer look at what we are doing. God does not call us to serve the world and neglect our families. Here's how we find the balance: Wisdom has to walk alongside of compassion, so that we are not serving one person at the expense of another. Therefore, we have to look at how our actions—even actions of service and compassion— might be causing us to neglect or otherwise hurt others.

G. K. Chesterton said, "To have a right to do a thing is not at all the same as to be right in doing it."

Dying to Our "Rights"

Dying to self not only enables us to serve others better, but it also brings peace and contentment into our own lives. Surrendering to Christ frees us from always feeling that we don't have enough, that we weren't treated fairly, that we should demand our rights. The unhappiest people in the world are those who feel as if the world owes them something.

For example, America was founded on the idea of liberty, but we have taken that to the extreme. Originally, the word meant "the right to do what is right." But this postmodern society has changed its meaning so that, for many people today, *liberty* is defined as "the right to do whatever I want to do." Even many Christians have adopted this idea. However, true liberty will not cost others *their* liberty.

The area in which most of us seem to want to hold on to our rights most tightly is in the area of forgiveness. When people do something to hurt us, we feel as if we have the right to hold a grudge. But, as followers of Christ, we must understand that the people who are the most blessed and happy are those who are continually filled with gratitude for their own forgiveness and who freely forgive others because they themselves have been forgiven.

When Peter asked Jesus how many times he should forgive a brother who sinned against him and questioned if seven times was sufficient, Jesus answered, "Not seven times, but seventy-seven times." Then He told Peter this story:

> The people who are most blessed and happy are those who are grateful for their own forgiveness and freely forgive others because they themselves have been forgiven.

Therefore, the kingdom of heaven is like a king who wanted to settle accounts with his servants. As he began the settlement, a man who owed him ten thousand talents [several million dollars] was brought to him. Since he was not able to pay, the master ordered that he and his wife and his children and all that he had be sold to repay the debt. The servant fell on his knees before him. "Be patient with me," he begged, "and I will pay back everything." The servant's master took pity on him, canceled the debt and let him go. But when that servant went out, he found one of his fellow servants who owed him a hundred denarii [a few dollars]. He grabbed him and began to choke him. "Pay back what you owe me!" he demanded. His fellow servant fell to his knees and begged him, "Be patient with me, and I will pay you back." But he refused. Instead, he went off and had the man thrown into prison until he could pay the debt. When the other servants saw what had happened, they were greatly distressed and went and told their master everything that had happened. Then the master called the servant in. "You wicked servant," he said, "I canceled all that debt of yours because you begged me to. Shouldn't you have had mercy on your fellow servant just as I had on you?" In anger his master turned him over to the jailers to be tortured, until he should pay back all he owed. This is how my heavenly Father will treat each of you unless you forgive your brother from your heart.

We might read this story and think, *How heartless, how ungrateful, how unloving could this man be? He was forgiven a huge debt and then turned around and threw a person in jail who owed him a measly amount. How could he be so unchanged by the mercy he had received?*

But if we think that, we have missed the point of the story. We are the ones who have been forgiven much. We should be asking ourselves, "Am I extending forgiveness to others?" We all have received such incredible grace. We are called to treat others with the same grace that Jesus has shown to us. There are so many things that God has given us through Christ that we don't deserve. He commands us to show that same mercy to others—to forgive as many times as they need to be forgiven.

We know from personal experience that this is not always easy to do. It's hard enough in marriage, but life in the band is kind of like being married to *four* other people. After ten years of working together and traveling together, sometimes it's hard to say, "I'm sorry." Sometimes it's hard to keep our mouths closed, but we have to extend to one another the grace that we have been given.

It can be a challenge to live out what we believe, but when it becomes difficult, we can look to the example of Jesus. His commitment to forgiving us took Him all the

> We are called to treat others with the same grace that Jesus has shown to us.

way to the cross. He loved us so much that He chose to literally die for us. It was so difficult for Him that twice He cried out to God to see if it were possible not to have to go through it. But because our forgiveness required that He do so, He did it.

If He was willing to make that kind of sacrifice for the sake of love, we should be willing to do the same. Our natural reaction is to become angry and resentful when we are wronged. But if we commit to working out our differences with people, as a sacrifice unto Christ, we often gain stronger and better relationships as a result.

Our song "Million Pieces" talks about the bitterness and other baggage that can build up within us, and how we are to just let it go instead of allowing it to fester in our hearts. We do this by committing the problem to God, asking Christ to give us His heart of forgiveness, and making a conscious decision to love as He loved. Then we are able to truly let these things go and find real freedom.

The Other Side of Sacrifice: Joy Unspeakable

If life is water, I was dry as the Tuscon dirt
If it's a gamble, I'd already lost my shirt
If it's a journey, I was dazed without a clue
I flipped a "U" back to the first love I
ever knew

You give me joy that's unspeakable
Your love for me is irresistible
You carried the cross and took my shame
You shine your light of amazing grace

Bowed and broken, everything's new
All that I need, you're like water to seed
And how your love, rights everything wrong
In my weakness
You're ever stronger, you're pulling me back
Where I belong

"Joy," *Shine: The Hits*

There is joy that awaits on the other side of the needle, when we've passed through the point of surrendering our rights and losing ourselves. When we finally squeeze through that impossible hole, made possible only by God's grace, then there is major joy waiting for us there. Jesus promises us in His Word that no one who has sacrificed for the kingdom's sake "will fail to receive many times as much in this age and, in the age to come, eternal life."

Joy is perhaps the Christian's biggest secret. It's our biggest secret because it's unspeakable. We can't really describe it. We can say the word, but it's something that can be experienced only on the other side of the needle. Joy is not found inside us; it's found as we empty ourselves in order to be filled with Christ. It's found as we seek His kingdom first. Joy is one of the "all these things" that is added to us.

The Bible says that Christ came to make our joy "complete." We talk about Christ coming and dying for our sins, about His being the great Mediator and "the way, the truth, and the life," but He also came to make our joy complete. That means that our joy will always be incomplete without Him. Joy comes from filling ourselves with Christ because the more we fill ourselves with Him, the less room we have for ourselves.

We all want joy, but we seem to want to obtain it by promoting ourselves instead of humbling ourselves. When Jesus said that those who love their life will lose it and those who lose their life will find it, maybe part of what He meant was that people will find or lose their joy in this life depending on whether or not they are surrendered to Christ.

Shine

Joy is a gift that our Creator wants to give us through His Son. We don't have a Father who wants us to sacrifice in order to make us sad. He wants us to sacrifice because He knows it will bring us joy. It's that upside-down kingdom again. C. S. Lewis said, "No soul that seriously and constantly desires joy will ever miss it. Those who seek find. To those who knock it is opened."

> God doesn't want us to
> sacrifice in order to make us
> sad, but because He knows it
> will bring us joy.

A Natural Part of Life

The principle of self-surrender can be applied to all our relationships. When we first practice and learn it in our homes, it will become a natural part of our lives. The Scripture says, "Let your light shine before men, that they may see your good deeds and praise your Father in heaven." To do good works, you have to be at a certain place in your own life. You have to be a servant, and what does that mean? It means to surrender your way of doing things and serve someone else out of reverence for Christ.

As this process occurs in our lives, our families and friends will notice the difference. Don't be surprised if they say, "You've changed. What's going on? You're so much more peaceful now. You're less temperamental, more

214

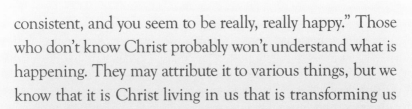

consistent, and you seem to be really, really happy." Those who don't know Christ probably won't understand what is happening. They may attribute it to various things, but we know that it is Christ living in us that is transforming us into new creations.

Phil describes how the process of surrender has been manifested in his own life:

> As I become more like Christ, my wife loves me more. It's kind of strange considering that I am becoming less. But she's loving me more because she's seeing that I'm becoming more in a different way. It's about following Christ and becoming who He wants you to be. It's so hard to explain. It's just so sweet and strange and upside-down.

Surrender is a continual process. Maybe in a few years, we'll look back to where we are now and think, "Wow! I was so immature then. I really didn't know the Lord the way I know Him now." And that's okay. Hopefully, that will be the case, for that is the way God intends it to work as we grow in Him and bear fruit for the kingdom. Even at the end of our lives, we'll be able to say, "There's still so much more that the Lord wants to show me."

Living and Growing in the Community of Believers

As we said earlier, it is not only our one-on-one relationship with the Lord that enables us to surrender to Christ and grow in His grace, but also the love of a nurturing Christian community. Paul wrote in Romans, "Just as each of us has one body with many members, and these members do not all have the same function, so in Christ we who are many form one body, and each member belongs to all the others." Paul was saying that all believers *belong* to one another as part of the same body of Christ, just as much as a person's arm or foot belongs to that person's body. Paul continued by describing the nature of the covenant community of believers:

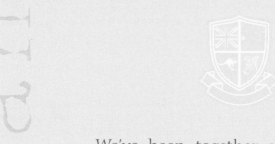

We've been together as a band for over ten years. We are brothers, and we love to do things together, like ride motorbikes. Sometimes, when we're on the bus, we'll start talking about a certain trip we took to the Baja Peninsula or when the bike blew up and all this kind of stuff. Those things are precious to me because of these incredibly wonderful memories of these guys that I'd do anything for. I'd give them the shirt off my back. In a thousand years' time, we're going to be saying, "Remember that time in the Baja Peninsula when we...?"

When people say, "All you need is God," or "All you need is Jesus," that is certainly true in regard to your salvation. But I really believe that there's something missing from that statement. We need each other. Why did God Almighty, our Creator, create beings? He didn't have to. He was God. He could have done anything. He could have created robots. Why did He create beings with free will? He wanted people. He wanted beings made in His image that He could share the rest of eternity with. Even God Almighty wants mates. He wants buddies. I really believe that. He wants to share His life with similar free-will beings. He wants relationship. And if that is what is good for my Creator, it's good for me, too, as a being created in His image.

We have different gifts, according to the grace given us. If a man's gift is prophesying, let him use it in proportion to his faith. If it is serving, let him serve; if it is teaching, let him teach; if it is encouraging, let him encourage; if it is contributing to the needs of others, let him give generously; if it is leadership, let him govern diligently; if it is showing mercy, let him do it cheerfully. Love must be sincere. Hate what is evil; cling to what is good. Be devoted to one another in brotherly love. Honor one another above yourselves. Never be lacking in zeal, but keep your spiritual fervor, serving the Lord. Be joyful in hope, patient in affliction, faithful in prayer. Share with God's people who are in need. Practice hospitality. Bless those who persecute you; bless and do not curse. Rejoice with those who rejoice; mourn with those who mourn. Live in harmony with one another. Do not be proud, but be willing to associate with people of low position. Do not be conceited. Do not repay anyone evil for evil. Be careful to do what is right in the eyes of everybody. If it is possible, as far as it depends on you, live at peace with everyone.

This is a picture of a body of believers who are committed both to Christ and to one another. Love and the other fruits of the Spirit are prominent. Each member has a valuable role to play in strengthening the others in the Lord and meeting the needs of the community. Encouragement and instruction in the Lord are provided so believers can grow and mature in their faith. The members not only support each other's weaknesses, but they also nurture each other's strengths.

What we learn from this passage of Scripture is that our relationships with God are not carried out in isolation. We need others to express God's love to us and to help us become all that God wants us to be. In addition, the major way we learn to love God Himself is by loving the members of His body. The apostle John emphasized this when he wrote:

If anyone says, "I love God," yet hates his brother, he is a liar. For anyone who does not love his brother, whom he has seen, cannot love God, whom he has not seen. And he has given us this command: Whoever loves God must also love his brother.

Seven Needs of Every Christian

One of the things we have been learning as a band is that it's one thing for us to be in ministry, but we are not a church unto ourselves. As individuals, we need to be connected to a community of believers by participating in a local church. In this way, we can minister to others on a one-to-one basis and be ministered to ourselves. There we can share the gifts that God has given to us, but also be discipled, so that we can continue to grow and mature in our faith.

Our growing understanding of our need to be in relationship with other believers has come from participating in several Bible studies given by our friend Pastor Ray McCollum. He called one of the studies, "Seven Needs of a Newsboy," which are actually needs that apply to all believers. He also gave a series entitled, "Corporate Destiny." What follows is the essence of those teachings.

Need #1
A Spiritual Family

First, we all need a spiritual family. Hebrews 11:8-10 tells us:

In the last couple of years, I really solidly started getting involved in my church and honestly recognizing my pastor as my pastor. That's caused an enormous change. There's really some strength, some power, in recognizing the delegates that God has put in your life to feed you, to minister to you, to help nurture you and make you grow. Being involved in church, becoming a member of my church, which I hadn't been before, has been a real instrument of change. Part of that change has come about because our church has a program in which we read particular Scriptures together. It's been really good. It's helped me to form my discipline in having my devotions. Going through this program, learning and studying the Bible with my church, which is the part of the body that I'm involved in, has been a real amazing time of growth for me.

By faith Abraham, when called to go to a place he would later receive as his inheritance, obeyed and went, even though he did not know where he was going. By faith he made his home in the promised land like a stranger in a foreign country; he lived in tents, as did Isaac and Jacob, who were heirs with him of the same promise. For he was looking forward to the city with foundations, whose architect and builder is God.

One of the marks of a true Christian is the desire to be with other believers. Abraham went out looking for a "city with foundations." This city refers to the people of God, the "city on a hill" whose light cannot be hidden. Abraham may not have known where he was going, but he knew what he was looking for and who was leading him.

We also should be looking for a spiritual family to be related to. When God created the world, He said that everything was good except for one thing. We read in Genesis, "The LORD God said, 'It is not good for the man to be alone. I will make a helper suitable for him.'" Human beings need to be in relationship with other human beings. This is especially important in today's world where disposable relationships are more common every day, whether in regard to marriage or friendship. It is a blessing to have lifelong friends. This can happen when we are in a spiritual family. In fact, that is where we gain eternal friendships.

How do we know what is the best spiritual family for us to be a part of when there are so many churches to choose from? Choosing a church home can sometimes be a difficult process. We had no choice about the natural families we were born into. We learned who our families were through our physical senses—by being held and nurtured by them, hearing their voices, and seeing their faces. But finding our spiritual family takes discernment because it will play a significant role in our growth and development as children of God. Here are six keys to finding your place in a local body of believers.

Being part of a local church is a commitment, a covenantal connection with other believers.

Understanding the Call to Community

Some people were practically "born" into their spiritual families. Their parents attended the same church all their lives, so it became their church home, also. However, our society has become very transient, and this is no longer the case for many people. When they move, they are put in the position of needing to find a new spiritual family. Other people have come to know Christ later in their lives or have drifted away from church for a while, and so they also are in search of home churches. The first question we should ask ourselves is, "Do I understand what it means to be joined to others in this way?" because being part of a local church is a commitment. It is a covenantal connection with other believers. When you realize that God is calling you to enter into this commitment with others, it is the right time for you to become part of a spiritual family.

A Feeling of Home

Have you ever gone out looking for a house to buy? You visit home after home. Most have their good points and their bad points, but if you are fortunate, when you walk into one, it will just *feel* like home. It's not perfect. You'd hoped it would be located on a cul-de-sac, and it's not. You wanted a two-car garage, but it has only one. You'd change other things if you could, but you knew when you saw it, and when you walked around inside it, that this was the one. You'd found your home.

A similar thing happens in finding the right church home. You visit a particular church, and maybe you think the music is too loud or too traditional. Maybe it has folding chairs, and you were looking for cushioned pews. However, when you walked inside, you felt the presence of the Lord. You can handle all the style differences because you have found *substance*. The Lord is there.

Shared Vision and Values

When you board an airplane, have you ever listened to the opening announcement? The flight attendant says something like, "Ladies and gentlemen, welcome aboard American Airlines flight 1347, non-stop service to Los Angeles." Why do the airlines do that? They do it because they have to. The FAA requires that they give a destination check. It's a final chance for someone to realize, "Hey, this plane is headed in a different direction than I want to go. Let me off!" Similarly, you need to know in what direction your church is headed. What is its vision? What are its core values?

Every family has its own set of values. Perhaps your family taught you never to lie. Maybe you had to check in at a certain time. When you went to a football game and the gang wanted to go out for pizza afterward, you had to call home. When your friends kidded you about it, did you say, "You can make fun of me, but if I don't call home, my parents will kill me. So I'm calling home!"? You did it because it was one of the principles that was taught and followed in your family.

Churches have core values, too. If you are going to participate in the life of the community, you need to know that you can embrace and support the church's vision and values. If you do not agree with them, it is the wrong spiritual home for you.

Trust and Respect for Leadership

As Christians, we are called to love everyone, but we aren't necessarily to *trust* everyone. Trust is something that is earned. People can't build a life together without trust.

Love is certainly vital to relationships, but trust allows us to make a long-term commitment to others that will endure.

We live in a time when it's more difficult to trust people in leadership because many of our leaders have betrayed our trust. Whether it's government employees who sell secrets to another country, politicians who are unfaithful to their spouses, or church leaders who break

---

> Love is vital to a relationship,
> but trust allows it to endure.

---

their vows to God and to His body, we are all affected by faithless acts of betrayal. The enemy has used these betrayals of trust to cause us to be suspicious of leadership in general. However, we can't function in community without trust. Even at the risk of being hurt, we must learn to trust our church family—especially those in leadership. This does *not* mean that we are to blindly offer our trust. We should check the leaders' "relational credit history."

Have you ever tried to borrow money? In order to get a loan, you have to fill out a credit history. You can't tell the bank officer, "I'm sorry. That's personal information.

It's none of your business how much money I make or what bills I owe." We shouldn't be offended when those questions are asked. That information is necessary for the bank to determine if we will be faithful in repaying a loan or if we are a bad risk.

In the same way, you need to know your leaders' backgrounds. Have they been faithful to their families, to their church members, to their commitment to God? No one is perfect; we all have our weaknesses. However, it is essential to know if, in the big issues of life, your leaders can be trusted.

Doctrinal Agreement

We don't have to agree with our church family on every small point of doctrine. However, it is essential to be in agreement on the "irreducible minimums," or foundational truths of the faith, such as the Virgin Birth; the Trinity; and the death, resurrection, and second coming of Jesus. Some things are fundamental to our faith, and we will never feel at home in our spiritual family if we are not in agreement on those points. Certain things are non-essentials, and we can be in unity with others without seeing every aspect of our faith from the same perspective. For instance, baptism is essential, but it is not as essential to agree on the *particulars* of baptism, such as whether to baptize in the name of Jesus or in the name of the Father, Son, and Holy Spirit. It is not that some of these points are irrelevant, but they don't have to keep us from being in fellowship with one another.

An Environment Conducive to Growth

When you are in your true spiritual family, your faith will be stretched. You will be challenged by the messages you hear from God's Word. It is within the body of Christ that we should be able to "grow up into him who is the Head, that is, Christ." Among our spiritual family, we will be fed the Word so that we can "grow in the grace and knowledge of our Lord and Savior Jesus Christ." That does not mean that we do not have a personal responsibility to study God's Word and to spend time in daily communion with Him. However, we should receive food from His table when we gather with our community of believers.

Need #2
Definition

In addition to needing a spiritual family, all believers need to know who they are in Christ. In Part III, we talked about defining moments, and that is part of what we are talking about here. But more specifically, this definition refers to the means that God uses to help us discover our spiritual identity.

His Word

First, God's Word reveals who we are. For example, 1 John 3:10 tells us that we are God's children if we do what is right and if we love our brothers. Romans 8:17 tells us that we are "heirs of God and co-heirs with Christ." Ephesians 2:10 explains that "we are God's workmanship, created in Christ Jesus to do good works, which God prepared in advance for us to do."

His Family

God also clarifies our image of ourselves through our spiritual family. Just as we identify ourselves in our natural families as father, mother, brother, or sister, our spiritual families help us to understand our position in the body of Christ, as we learn in 1 Corinthians 12.

> Our need to be a part of the family of God is as real and as important as our place in an earthly family.

Some people feel, "I'm a Christian, so that makes me part of the family of God. I don't need to become connected with a community of believers." That is like saying you don't need a natural family because you are in the family of man. The second part of the statement is true. We all do belong to the larger human family. However, that alone is a poor substitute for knowing one's mother and father and brothers and sisters.

Definition requires context. For instance, you may be a father, but when you go to your job, you may be the boss. You may be a wife, but when you visit your parents, you are their daughter. We understand who we are by where we are, what we are doing, and with whom we are in relationship. Therefore, within the context of a church family, you can discover and develop the gifts that God has given you to use to further His kingdom on earth.

Spiritual Fathers

The New Testament tells of a centurion who came to Christ to ask the Lord to heal his servant, who was paralyzed. This centurion understood authority. He was a man of authority himself because he had a hundred men under him. He not only had faith in Christ, but he also had faith that Christ was a delegate of God. In other words, he understood that Jesus had authority of His own but that He was also under God's authority. Because this centurion accepted Christ's authority and believed in it, Jesus was able to heal his servant without even going to where he was.

In contrast, when Jesus went to His hometown, the people there didn't believe He was a delegate of God. They saw Him merely as Joseph's son, the son of a carpenter. The Bible says, "He did not do many miracles there because of their lack of faith."

In the body of Christ, God uses spiritual fathers, His representatives or delegates, to help us mature in our faith and discover our spiritual gifts. In order to accept their guidance, we have to believe that they have been brought into our lives to minister to us and to help us grow. This is something that God will confirm to us as we rely on His leading. Again, the matter of trust is important here. We are to give our leaders the respect they deserve, but we also are to test their lives and characters before trusting in their leadership.

Need #3
Inspiration

Third, every believer needs spiritual inspiration. Remember the story of David killing the Philistine Goliath with a stone and a slingshot? When the young shepherd boy was brought to King Saul, he still had the giant's head in his hands. After David had finished talking with Saul, Saul's son Jonathan "became one in spirit with David, and he loved him as himself." Jonathan was inspired by David, and a bond grew between them that was as close as that of any brothers.

There is something significant about being inspired by someone who can do things in a greater or better way than we can. This is one reason watching sports is so popular. We are moved by seeing the level of ability someone has achieved that is beyond anything we can do ourselves. Often seeing an athlete reach such a level inspires us to try harder in our own efforts.

When we are part of a spiritual family, we can inspire others in their service to God as well as be inspired by them. We need to be around people who love God and do great things for Him. The writer of Hebrews said, "Remember your leaders, who spoke the word of God to you. Consider the outcome of their way of life and imitate their faith."

We should look for role models in the church who have followed God well and whose lives have been blessed because of their steadfast obedience. For example, we should look for couples who have loving, long-lasting marriages and successful business people who have maintained their integrity. We need the inspiration that we can find within our own spiritual family.

Need #4
Moral Accountability

Fourth, all believers need moral accountability. When Adam and Eve sinned, they hid from God, but He called to them and said, "Where are you?" He wasn't asking for their geographical location. Their hiding behind a bush didn't confuse God. No, He was saying, "Do you know where you are in relation to Me? Do you know what you've done? Give Me an account. Tell Me what happened." Of course, He knew what they had done, but He wanted them to confess it to Him. However, instead of being forthright about their actions, Eve blamed the serpent and Adam blamed Eve. Humankind has followed their example ever since. We work hard trying to justify our sins, whereas God wants us to have true accountability for our actions.

For our own good, God wants us to keep a short account with Him. We can go to Him daily and pray as David prayed, "Search me, O God, and know my heart; test me and know my anxious thoughts. See if there is any offensive way in me, and lead me in the way everlasting." If you do not keep a clean record with God, you will start to accumulate spiritual and emotional baggage in your life.

> We work hard to justify our sins, but God wants us to be accountable for our actions.

Just because a heavenly lightning bolt hasn't struck you down doesn't mean that God isn't aware of your sin. To keep your heart pure, stay in close relationship with your heavenly Father.

Vertical accountability with God is vital. However, we also need horizontal accountability with other people. That doesn't mean that we are accountable to *everyone* in a general sense. It means that we need one or two mature and trusted Christians with whom we can discuss our spiritual problems and needs. So often, when well-known people have fallen into sin in a public way, the root of the problem has been that they had no accountability to anyone. Their problems started out small and in secret, but there was no one with whom they could address them.

There was no real practical accountability, so the secret just grew and grew and, like a ticking bomb that is not defused, it exploded. The explosion devastated many lives, and other people were left to pick up the pieces.

We need to realize that part of sin's power is in its secrecy. There is something about getting our failures into the light that seems to defuse their power. As long as your sin or failure is your secret, as long as you are doing it in private, it seems to have a great power over you. But

Part of sin's power is its secrecy.
We each need a mature Christian
with whom we can discuss our
spiritual problems and needs.

if you can take the courageous step of faith to become accountable and tell a pastor or elder or someone who loves you and is walking in victory that you need some help, you are taking a huge step toward overcoming that problem. The enemy of your soul wants you to keep your sins private because his hold over you becomes greater when you do.

Most people, deep down, hunger to be able to talk to another person about their greatest concerns. However, they also fear it because they don't know how others will react or what they will do with the information. This

may be one reason for the popularity of Internet "chat rooms." People feel they can expose their needs and fears to someone anonymous whom they will never meet and who doesn't have any power over them.

Yet confessing to someone in person, someone who knows and loves you, will make a significant difference in receiving help and healing. It also is important for you to know that the person you are confessing to will give you an honest assessment of the problem because many people will not tell you the truth. Either they don't want to hurt your feelings or they don't want to deal with your problems. That is why it is very freeing to know there are one or two people you can go to and confess your struggle and ask for help without being rejected, and receive the kind of candid feedback that we all need if we are going to be honest and real. Asking for their prayers and knowing that they will be following up with you can bring victory.

Sometimes we are unable to see our own shortcomings. Therefore, another important aspect of accountability is asking a trusted counselor who knows you well to help you see areas in your life that need to be worked on. Paul wrote, "Examine yourselves to see whether you are in the faith; test yourselves." Asking for help in this area doesn't mean we're inviting people to take potshots at us. However, when we are willing to be vulnerable and teachable with someone who has our best spiritual interests in mind, God can use that level of accountability to help us to mature in our faith.

What keeps people from wanting to be held accountable? There are at least four enemies, and the first one goes back to what we have already talked about: people's tendency to hide their sins. We can invent dozens of reasons for why we don't need to be accountable. We can say things like these: "I got hurt once." "I don't know anyone well enough to tell my personal concerns to." "I'm a private person. I couldn't reveal my hidden secrets to anyone." "I don't have the time to seek out a relationship like this." "I wouldn't know where to start."

None of these reasons or excuses needs to keep us from the benefits of accountability. What can you do to overcome your fears, step out in faith, and find someone to whom you can be held accountable? First, you have to seek God's direction in finding the right person. Think about people who really love you, people whose spiritual lives you respect, and whom you trust to be accepting and confidential in what you tell them. Say to them, "I know you're busy, but would you be willing to spend some time with me—whatever you can spare, I'll work around your schedule—and coach me in some spiritual matters, and let me learn from you? If you would be willing to do that, it would mean a lot to me." Most people will readily agree to do it. In fact, the busier they are, the more likely they will be willing to do it. They have probably asked for the same thing for themselves. These people can become a mirror for you to help you see yourself in a true light. You can also sit down with those who are your closest friends and say, "I want to be a better person in the Lord. What do you see in me that needs to be worked on?"

Again, the area of trust is important. We don't go to just anyone and ask him to mentor us. Usually that comes after years of knowing someone or of knowing his character, so that you know you can trust that person. If you are faithful in asking God to help you find a spiritual delegate,

Having someone to hold you accountable
is like having a mirror to help you
see yourself in a true light.

or mentor, He will be faithful in leading you to people who are trustworthy and who are gifted in mentoring. You should be part of a spiritual family that has people in leadership whom you respect and in whom you can confide. The writer of Hebrews said, "Obey your leaders and submit to their authority. They keep watch over you as men who must give an account."

We should be aware that the enemy sometimes uses people's personality differences to prevent them from being real with one another. Some of us are basically shy and introverted. It goes against our nature to seek someone out and ask for help—even when we know we need to do it. Others of us are loud, maybe even intimidating to others. People are afraid to approach us, fearful of being belittled or ignored, even when that is the last thing we would do to them.

Personality differences can often fuel people's fears of rejection. We think, "If people knew what I was struggling with, they wouldn't think much of me." Yet some people who outwardly seem to have it all together may actually

---

God's purpose is to conform us to His image. Are you more like Christ today than you were yesterday?

---

be hurting, hiding their fears and their personal struggles with sin. If we want to develop godly lives, we must look past our fears and be willing to be held accountable to other Christians. We need to look beyond personality differences and get to know other people so we can receive spiritual strength from one another.

Differences in age can also keep people from feeling as if they can connect with one another. However, there is a wealth of knowledge that older people can offer younger people. And younger believers can remind more mature believers of the fresh joy that comes from knowing we are loved and forgiven by God. We have to realize that sometimes a younger person can offer spiritual insight to those who are older.

God's purpose is to conform us to His image. It is a life-long process of building His character in us. To cooperate with this process, we should ask ourselves, "What do I do when nobody is looking? Who am I when no one else is around? Am I more like Christ today than I was yesterday? In spite of my failings, am I still trying to serve God?"

God wants to "scandal-proof" us. He wants His character to be revealed in our thoughts, our words, and our actions. He helps us to become more like Him as we read His Word, pray, examine our own lives, and use other Christians as mirrors to help us see ourselves. They not only point out our blind spots, but also help us to see the good things in our lives and characters that we sometimes overlook. The flower of Christ's nature and character will blossom forth in an atmosphere of moral accountability with someone we trust.

Need #5
Trustworthy Counsel/Confirmation

Fifth, every believer needs trustworthy counsel. Strong marriages are built on trust. Close families are built on trust. Great businesses are built on trust. Significant ministries are built on trust. The kingdom of God is built on trust. Knowing that you are receiving good counsel is vital to transformation and growth because if you don't trust what you are hearing, you won't apply it to your life and it won't benefit you. In some ways, the more we are able to receive good counsel from others, the more we may be able to receive from God Himself and vice versa.

One of the most important aspects of receiving good counsel is confirmation. In other words, when three people tell you the same thing about yourself, that is usually confirmation about the truth of it. Counsel also has to line up with the Word of God. We should not be willing to receive something that isn't in harmony with God's Word. In addition, the Holy Spirit will bring conviction to our own hearts that what someone is saying is true. When these three things converge, it is counsel we can trust.

Need #6
Protection and Covering

Sixth, every believer needs a spiritual covering. The word *headship* is often misunderstood in today's culture. It does *not* describe the relationship between a slave and his master. It implies more of a guardianship. A faithful shepherd watching out for his sheep is a good picture of true protection and covering.

We must look to those who are under authority themselves in order to find real protection. We should never submit to someone who is not under authority. Wolves are loose in our world, and we need the Good Shepherd to protect us. He uses godly undershepherds to protect us and to keep us on the right path.

As we submit to those in authority who are submitted to God's authority, we can be comforted in knowing that faithful believers are watching out for us. Just as the shepherd's rod and staff were there to guide and protect the sheep, we can be helped in our walk as we listen to the Good Shepherd and the undershepherds He uses to guide and protect us.

The Good Shepherd and His undershepherds are there with rod and staff to protect us.

Need #7
Maturity

Seventh, we need to be connected to others in the body of Christ in order to grow and mature in our faith. The gifts that Christ has given His church are meant to be at work in our lives. We discover and exercise these gifts in the context of our interactions with others in the body. Our relationships with other believers also enable us to mature personally and spiritually. Learning to live in harmony with others requires growth—surrendering ourselves and learning to extend grace and forgiveness. We will grow primarily in the context of our relationships with others because, on our own, it's harder for us to recognize our selfishness and lack of love.

If I hadn't met my wife, I would be lost. God has used her massively. When I say "lost," I don't mean eternally. I will always believe that Christ is who He said He is. I believe that He's given me the grace to believe that. However, I might have missed what He really wanted for me. Through marriage, He has sustained me spiritually. The same thing is true of certain friendships. He has sustained me through "iron sharpening iron." There are certain men who have been friends and mentors to me, and I think, "But by the grace of God, these men wouldn't have been there," and I would have been only half the person that I really need to be.

As we think over these needs of all believers, let's ask ourselves these questions and pray that God will enable us to answer *yes* to all of them:

1. Have I found my spiritual family?

2. Can I truly say I have been "defined" by those in my spiritual family who really know me and understand my gifts and calling?

3. Do I have men and women (locally, in my church) whose lives inspire me to a closer walk with Christ?

4. Can I truly say that I am morally accountable to a local spiritual leader, someone who loves me unconditionally and to whom I can be totally honest about my life and my secret struggles?

5. Can I truly say that I am under God-given spiritual authority and that I receive God's delegates in my life? Do I see the character of the Good Shepherd in the undershepherds in my life?

6. Do I feel covered and protected by my pastor and my church? Is my family spiritually "safe"? Do I have those in my life who know me well enough to defend me if I were to be falsely accused?

7. Can I truthfully say that I am vitally connected with spiritual leadership and with the church of Jesus Christ and that I know I am maturing and growing in my faith and fruitfulness as a disciple?

Preserving Unity in the Church

The apostle Paul wrote,

Be completely humble and gentle; be patient, bearing with one another in love. Make every effort to keep the unity of the Spirit through the bond of peace. There is one body and one Spirit—just as you were called to one hope when you were called.

One of the most important ways we reflect the character of Christ in our lives is by extending His love and grace to those in His body. This is why it is essential to understand the ways in which the "unity of the Spirit" can be undermined, and to commit ourselves to living a life of love.

Envy

Envy will tear apart relationships quicker than anything else. Envy manifests itself in attitudes that demand credit and attention. The devil knows that if he can come in among people and get envy or jealousy going, then he has established a foothold. To be one in the Spirit, we have to truly rejoice and be happy for other people's successes. Only through Christ as our Everything is this possible. If our friends receive a blessing, we ought to be thrilled for them. If we can't rejoice when other people are successful, it will drive a wedge between us and them. If we become envious and jealous of one another, we will never be in unity because that bitter spirit will always run underneath the surface of our relationships. The Bible says, "Rejoice with those who rejoice." If you want to have the kind of unity that keeps relationships together forever, envy has to be dealt with immediately.

Do you remember why Cain killed his brother? It was out of envy. God accepted his brother Abel's offering, but He rejected Cain's offering. When God saw that Cain was angry, He told him, "If you do what is right, will you not be accepted? But if you do not do what is right, sin is crouching at your door; it desires to have you, but you must master it." Instead of repenting, Cain allowed his envy to grow to the point that he killed his brother. In the first chapters of the Bible, we see the tragic results of how envy literally destroyed unity among brothers.

Envy can ruin relationships and destroy lives. If we want to walk together in unity with our physical and spiritual families, we have to eliminate the spirit of envy.

Illegitimacy

Another hindrance to unity is illegitimacy. In Hebrews 12:8, *illegitimacy* does not refer to being born out of wedlock but being unwilling to receive correction. God corrects us, or chastens us, when we are His children. He disciplines us out of love to keep us from harm because He is our Father. But His Word says, "If you are not disciplined (and everyone undergoes discipline), then you are illegitimate children and not true sons."

Therefore, if you refuse to be corrected when it is called for, you have the spirit of illegitimacy, and wherever that occurs, unity is disrupted.

Suppose someone were running rampant through the church body, gossiping, slandering, dividing, and criticizing, and nobody corrected that person. What would happen? Would there be unity in a church like that? At some point, someone has to go and say, in love, "You have to stop acting like this. You can't keep slandering and gossiping. Your behavior is hurting the body of Christ."

If we are going to have unity, there has to be proper correction—and it has to be received. That's why we need pastors and elders. We have to have someone who can lovingly and objectively confront wrong attitudes and bad behavior.

Sometimes we are at fault, and we don't even recognize it. That is when somebody whom we have recognized as an authority has to step in, and that person has to correct us. It's not fun at the time, but it will enable us to grow in the Lord. The Bible says, "No discipline seems pleasant at the time, but painful. Later on, however, it produces a harvest of righteousness and peace for those who have been trained by it." Being able to accept correction when we need it will help us to maintain unity in our relationships.

Offenses

A third enemy to unity is offenses. Jesus said, "Woe to the world because of offenses! For offenses must come, but woe to that man by whom the offense comes!" Another way of saying that is, "How dreadful it will be for you if you are the one who causes someone else to sin."

Offenses occur when somebody says something or does something that wounds us emotionally. Jesus said that offenses are going to happen, but He tells us in Matthew 18 how to deal with them. He's very specific; it's very clear. If you don't deal with the problem in a biblical way, it will get worse. Offenses left to fester will destroy unity.

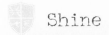

We all have had times when we put the proverbial foot in our mouths. We need to apologize to people, even when we unintentionally say something that offends them. These are offenses that have become stumbling blocks and are keeping us from being in relationship with one another.

The Greek word for offense is *skandalon*. The actual word refers to the trigger on a trap, as in an animal trap. If someone says something or does something, and you let it offend you, it is as if a trap snaps shut on your spirit, and this prevents you from growing in the Lord. Some people who have been hurt or offended have not grown in their spirits for years. If you can't deal with offenses properly, you won't stay married, you won't stay in a business partnership, you won't keep lasting friendships, and you won't stay in the same church with the person who has offended you. Or, if you do stay, you will be miserable and will cause others around you to be miserable, as well. Offenses that are ignored or not dealt with in a Christlike manner will cause you to stumble, and they will fracture unity. The positive side to dealing with offenses is that if you can reconcile them successfully, something wonderful happens. Your friendship, your bond, with the other person will be closer than ever.

In addition, it is through offenses that we discover what is really inside our spirits. How we handle being hurt reveals our character. We also reveal our character in the way that we receive correction. Too often, our first response is to be defensive. We says things like, "What about you? I've noticed that you need to work on a few things." A spirit that retaliates destroys unity, and the blessings that come with unity are thwarted. But a humble spirit retains both unity and its blessings.

Disregard

The fourth hindrance to unity is failing to accept those whom God has placed around you. When God leads you into relationships with people, such as friendships, marriage, a ministry, or a church, He brings you together sovereignly. That doesn't mean that you are going to be best friends with everyone you're around. We all have certain people who are special to us—people who enjoy the things we enjoy, people with whom we relate well. But God does not want us to pick and choose people with whom we associate, selecting some and disregarding others. We need to learn to walk in unity even with people whom we might not have chosen to be close to on our own.

Have you ever been put together with someone whom you would not have chosen for a friend? Maybe when you first met that person, you weren't very impressed. Later on, however, you became close friends, and that friend brought more blessings into your life than you would ever have imagined. Sometimes God will use the people who rub us the wrong way to bless and change us the most.

Infiltration

A fifth obstacle to unity is the enemy's infiltration. The devil hates unity, and he'll do anything to destroy it. His primary weapon is accusation. The Bible calls him the "accuser." How does the devil work? Well, have you ever said something and had your words turned against you? Someone totally misunderstood what you intended because the accuser was telling him that you meant something else. Or it can go the other way. When someone says something to you, the enemy will cause you to hear something different from what the person intended. If you talk it through with the other person and clarify what was really intended, you will invariably find out that, while the other person said something quite innocent, what you heard was a spirit of accusation.

For example, perhaps a couple is walking through the mall, and the wife sees something she likes and says, "Oh, I'd like to have that." Her husband responds, "You don't need that." Or they are out driving and she sees a house with a swimming pool, and she says, "Isn't that nice!" Her husband responds, "We don't need a swimming pool; do you know how much they cost?" Their conversations turn into arguments because the accuser is at work.

The woman is just commenting on things she finds attractive, but the enemy is whispering in her husband's ear, "You aren't a good provider. If you were, you could buy her what she wants." The man becomes defensive because he feels attacked. His wife is saying one thing, but he is hearing something else, and that is driving a wedge between their unity.

We can learn to listen with the ear of a disciple, which is a disciplined ear. We can actually learn to recognize the voice of the accuser. Just as a dog can hear a whistle at a high pitch, we can train ourselves to hear the enemy's accusing voice. Then the Lord can help us talk things out with one another so that the enemy will not be able to destroy our unity.

Disloyalty

A further barrier to unity is disloyalty. Loyalty means being faithful to people even when they are not present. Any man can be faithful to his wife when she's standing right there with him. The question is whether he is faithful when she is not around. Similarly, we need to be faithful to others in the church body, even when no one we know is around. That's the test of loyalty. If you really want to put your own character to the acid test, if you really want to walk in unity, then you have to say, "I'm going to be loyal. That means I won't talk negatively about somebody when he or she is not present. I'm not going to cross that line anymore."

If we want to have solid friendships, great marriages, thriving businesses, and Spirit-filled churches; if we want to be great in the kingdom, then we must walk in unity. The blessings are incredible when we do. The battle may be hard, but the blessings will make the victory all the sweeter.

God Makes Christians; We Are to Make Disciples

The Lord calls us to mature in our faith not only for our own spiritual growth, but also for the benefit of others in His body. He wants us to come to a point where we can give as well as receive spiritual wisdom and knowledge in the ways of the Lord.

When Jesus gave us important instructions just before He ascended to heaven, He didn't tell us to go make Christians, because only the Holy Spirit can draw people to Christ. However, He did tell us to go and make *disciples*:

> Go and make disciples of all nations, baptizing them in the name of the Father and of the Son and of the Holy Spirit, and teaching them to obey everything I have commanded you. And surely I am with you always, to the very end of the age.

God wants to use *us* to make disciples. Remember when Jesus spoke Lazarus back to life? He prayed, and God raised Lazarus from the dead. When Lazarus came out of the tomb, he was bound up in his grave clothes. Jesus said to those standing nearby, "Take off the grave clothes and let him go." There are some things that God does for us. However, there are other things He calls us to do for one another. Again, making Christians is God's part. Making disciples is ours.

First, if we are going to make disciples, we have to make sure we are being discipled ourselves. We have to "grow up" so we can become "spiritual fathers." Paul said to the church at Corinth, "Even though you have ten thousand guardians in Christ, you do not have many fathers." What can we learn from Paul in our generation?

Only the Holy Spirit can draw
people to Christ.

Paul was indicating that many of us will say to others, "I'll love you. I'll encourage you. I'll give you some good advice. We can even have a Bible study, and I hope it will bless you. But don't ask me to go beyond that."

When we lead people to the Lord, but then don't provide them with spiritual fathering, or discipling, we often lose them. Not many of us are willing to take the time to say to a new Christian, "You may be fifty years old, but you're a newborn, spiritually speaking. Let's get together and talk about repentance and the lordship of Christ and the gifts of the Spirit. Let's talk about what it means to be a follower of the Lord." People need spiritual fathers (and mothers) who will lead them to their Father in heaven.

If we're going to make disciples, we need faithful fathers and submitted sons. As we mature in the Lord, we should be functioning as both fathers who help others grow and sons who continue to learn from mature believers. In other words, if we're going to make disciples, we need each other. None of us matures alone. Staying alone is a sure recipe for remaining a babe in Christ. Every passage in the New Testament about maturing in our faith is always in the context of growing in the body of Christ. There's no growing up apart from relationships.

As a band, we minister to many people every year, but we can't make disciples from the stage. Making disciples means we have to get involved in people's lives in a real, direct way. The contact we have with people in our church and in our neighborhoods is where significant long-lasting spiritual growth will take place. The same is true for all believers, because this is God's design for us.

Discipleship means living one day at a time as though Jesus were near, near in time, near in place, the witness of our motives, our speech, our behavior. As indeed he is.

—Brennan Manning

Part V

Light for the Land
of Shadow

*The people walking in darkness have seen
a great light; on those living in the land of
the shadow of death a light has dawned.*

—Isaiah 9:2

As we lift up our hands
As we call on your name
Will you visit this place
By your mercy and grace
Holy, holy is his name alone

It is you
We adore
It is you
Praises are for
Only you
The heavens declare
It is you
It is you

"It Is You"
Thrive

Let your light shine before men, that they may see your good deeds and praise your Father in heaven.

—Matthew 5:16

No matter what your occupation or calling in life—
whether you're a pastor, a missionary, or someone
who checks water meters all day—it's people that
count. God has you where you are to touch the lives
of those who cross your path. God has you where you
are to hold your light high, like a city on a hill.
—Ron Mehl

What was it about Jesus that caused people to be drawn to Him? It was obvious to all that He was living a holy and righteous life. Why was it that the people you would think would have found Him hardest to approach—the outcasts, the forgotten, the people on the lowest levels of acceptable society—felt welcome in His presence?

The main reason is that *He understood and loved people.* He purposefully sought people out and ministered to them in their everyday activities and lives. They responded to His approachability, honesty, warmth, and humor. He had compassion on them and met not only their spiritual needs, but also their physical and emotional needs. He lived a Gospel that showed that God cares about the whole person—spirit, soul, and body—and wants to meet all the needs in people's lives. His message wasn't dependent on how people reacted to it; His unconditional love remained the same regardless of what people did.

People know it when they meet someone who truly understands and loves them. Trust immediately builds, and a relationship can develop. So to shine—to draw people to the light of Jesus—we must come to understand and love others in the everydayness of life, just as Jesus did. This is how we truly engage the culture with the Gospel of the kingdom. No matter what people do and no matter what they believe, a living demonstration of love and sacrifice can break through the barriers they have set up against God.

To shine, we must come to understand and love others in the everydayness of life—just as Jesus did.

In this section, we want to explore some of the things that prevent us from being a light for Christ in the world, as well as some of the practical ways we can show the compassion of Christ to others. We've included several stories about how these things have made a particular impact in our own lives—transforming our understanding of what it means to be the change we want to see. All of us are learning about this process, and it's through these experiences that we have come to know more about allowing the light of Christ to shine through us.

The first area we'll look at is the attitudes we have toward those in the world.

Attitudes toward the World

Judging Others

One of the main reasons we don't approach others with the love of Christ is because we fail to remember how easy it would be for us to be in their place. This truth hit home to Peter one night a few years ago.

We had finished a concert and were on the bus traveling to the next city on our tour. Usually, after doing a show, we still have a lot of adrenaline pumping, a lot of energy, so we end up staying up late into the night. We're like brothers, so we were wrestling and roughhousing with each other and having a good time. Later on, at about three o'clock in the morning, we pulled into a truck stop. When I got out, I noticed a young couple standing next to a pickup truck that was parked nearby. The girl was fairly young, and both of them had been drinking pretty hard, so that they were out of it, just wasted. They got into the truck and pulled out, tires squealing, nearly crashing right there at the gas station.

I remember thinking something condemning at the time, like, "Ah, man, what are these idiots doing? They're drinking and driving, and she's going to end up like this, and he's going to end up like that," and so on. But as soon as I stepped back onto the bus, I felt like I had been hit in the chest with something; it took my breath away. And then these words came into my mind: "But for the grace of God, that would be *you*."

Instantly, my judgmental attitude disappeared, and my heart went out to them. My perspective completely changed. That was when the meaning of the famous phrase, "There but for the grace of God, go I" was really revealed to me.

When we take on an attitude that we're better than others, we're holding on to pride rather than losing ourselves for the sake of Christ. Even while we're saying, "But for the grace of God, there go I," we could be thinking we're better than the person we're referring to. Sometimes we look at people who are living a foolish and dangerous lifestyle, and we say, "They deserve what they get." But we don't realize what we're saying. The question is, Where would any of us be if God gave us what we deserved? Since He has extended grace to us, we need to extend grace to others. It's like the lyrics of one of our songs, "We don't always get what we deserve, but we get what we don't deserve."

Prejudging Others

Sometimes it isn't judging people's actions but judging what we *think* they will do that prevents us from reaching out to them. We're hesitant to show people the love of Christ because we assume they automatically don't want to have anything to do with us. We think they've already formed opinions about us before even giving us a chance. Phil describes how he became aware of this in his own life:

I live in a town that is very conservative. Peter and Duncan both live there, too. It's a little community, and it's kind of neat. A lot of older, more traditional people live there.

And then there's me.

I walk through my town with long hair and whatever clothes I happened to throw on, pretty much looking like a freak to most of the people around there. In the past, when I was out walking, I'd think things like, "That guy really thinks I'm some kind of hippie, and he won't want to talk to me. I don't think I'll say hi to him." So I sort of kept my head lowered as I walked down the sidewalk.

After doing this for a while, I suddenly realized that I had been believing a lie. I hadn't even given people a chance to talk to me. I had just assumed they wouldn't want to. So now, when I walk down the sidewalk, I say hi to absolutely *everybody*, even if they don't say hi back, and I've gotten to know everybody in town.

Somehow we think other people will be intimidated by us or won't receive love from us because they don't quite understand who we are. We think they will take us on face value. That's really wrong. Reaching out to my neighbors was a challenge for me until I realized something: If I'm scared that my neighbors are going to take me at face value, that they're going to judge me, that they aren't going to allow me to talk with them and get to know them so that we can become friends, then I'm probably wrestling with the same issues they are. I'm taking *them* at face value. Sometimes our fears and misgivings spin around and look us back in the face.

My neighbors have been observing me for the past three years, and now, over the last little while, it's like they're all coming out of their shells and really wanting to know what it is that's going on. Not just whether or not I've been on tour or not. So it's kind of fun. I'm beginning to see that, slowly, all my neighbors trust me a lot more than they did when I first moved in. It's good, because they know who I am, and they're beginning to understand what it is that I do and how it equates to my life and that the two match. I'm really enjoying seeing that my neighbors know what it is that I do and know that I'm a Christian. I'm seeing the fruit of living a life based on Christ and now my neighbors are beginning to see it. So that's kind of cool.

Sometimes to shine and make them wonder what you've got takes a bit of time and a bit of patience. To shine, for me, personally, means to have an effect on my neighbors whether I am aware of it or not. It's not important for me to be on a big old stage with lots of lights and all this wonderful stuff, unless it's happening in my neighborhood.

We are Christ's body, so we're walking ambassadors for Christ here on earth. It's our job to just love. Sometimes it takes going out on a limb and being prepared to be shot down or to be thought of as a bit of a fool or an eccentric or Jesus freak or hippie or whatever. But I don't worry about that anymore.

 Shine

When we think that we have nothing in common with people in the world and that they wouldn't want to get to know us, thick barriers are put up between us—obstacles that block out the light of Christ.

> Sometimes to shine and make
> them wonder what you've got
> takes a bit of time and a
> bit of patience.

Feeling "Persecuted"

Another attitude that blocks the light of Christ between us and others is more subtle: It is the feeling of being "persecuted." Jesus did say that those who follow Him will be rejected by the world:

> "I tell you the truth," Jesus replied, "no one who has left home or brothers or sisters or mother or father or children or fields for me and the gospel will fail to receive a hundred times as much in this present age (homes, brothers, sisters, mothers, children and fields—and with them, persecutions) and in the age to come, eternal life."

However, sometimes we think we're being persecuted for the Gospel when, in reality, people are rejecting our *presentation* of the message rather than the message itself. For example, when we present certain truths, but communicate them in a way that is devoid of the grace of God, it sounds like condemnation in the ears of the people hearing them. Then, when people respond negatively to this attitude in us, we say to ourselves, "I'm getting walked on by the world."

> When we try to share the
> truths of God without the
> grace of God, it can sound
> like condemnation.

The fact is, no one responds well to a person who has a "holier than thou attitude"—even those who agree with the message itself! There was no one who was holier than Jesus, yet His was not a boastful or self-centered holiness. His truth penetrated the hearts of His hearers because it was untainted by pride or resentment. It was pure light and truth. Again, only when we surrender to Him can His clear light shine to others. Even when we serve others with pure motives, we may well get walked on. However, we can't take it personally, or we will cut off the light from the people around us.

Our Approach to the World

The second area we'll look at are the methods we often use to bring the message of the Gospel to the world. Often, we try to argue others into agreeing with us, as if the logic of our words will convince people. However, even when certain people are convinced, they may stubbornly reject the message because they feel they've been "shown up."

The apostle Paul said, "My message and my preaching were not with wise and persuasive words, but with a demonstration of the Spirit's power, so that your faith might not rest on men's wisdom, but on God's power." Even God's Word can come across as "men's wisdom" to people if it is not also revealed to them through God's Spirit. Peter describes how, even though we can appreciate Christian thinking and learning, God is showing him that when he himself is "taken out of the way," the Holy Spirit can work in people's hearts in some amazing ways. We can call the Holy Spirit's work *revelation* rather than *argumentation*:

The Holy Spirit seems to work best when we're not in the way. For example, when I go out and speak at concerts or to youth group leaders, I've found that the times when I feel as if I have just fumbled everything—and that seems to happen a lot, because I'm not a public speaker— the times when I didn't have my ducks in a row and I just seemed to mess everything up, surprisingly, were the times when I saw the most evidence of the Spirit's workings.

I got into studying Christian apologetics for a while. I liked reading G. K. Chesterton, who wrote *The Everlasting Man* and *Orthodoxy*. I wasn't interested in debating with people as much as I just had a love for it. It was a help in examining my own heart. I had some questions about certain aspects of our faith that I needed to have answered. I still enjoy reading Christian classics, and they help strengthen my faith a lot. But I don't talk about theology with others as much as I used to, because I have come to understand that there are definitive essentials of the faith, and then there are the nonessentials. A. W. Tozer said, and this is a paraphrase, that some people choose to believe rather than to know. There are people you run into like that, and I love those people. They have just chosen to believe the Gospel through simple faith in Jesus, and they don't need a deep theological treatise about it. It reminds me of what Jesus said: We're even more blessed than those who knew Jesus while He was on earth, because we've believed in Him even though we haven't seen Him.

I think that's where the Holy Spirit comes in, and this speaks volumes because, in the end, we cannot *prove* that

God exists. When you go into a battle with someone about theology, you're not really going to win someone; you're not going to shine by proving to them that God exists. I have come to a point in my life of just believing by faith. I got tired of looking at programs discussing whether or not Noah's ark had been found, and things like that, because there's never anything conclusive about them. In the end, what is following Christ all about? It's about faith, isn't it? And faith is the evidence of things not seen.

The Holy Spirit is a Revealer. I pray for revelation through the Scriptures, and God answers that. I think that is the key. Tozer says that the Holy Spirit takes God's truths from the book of apologetics and transfers them to the human heart. He does that with believers, and He also does it for those who need to come to Christ.

I saw an amazing example of this when we played a show at the Rock and Roll Hall of Fame. People came up to us afterward and said how much it had touched them. I *know* that was the Holy Spirit because, later, when I watched the footage, I wasn't impressed. There was no segue; we just went from one song to another. At the end of the show, I felt that it was the worst show we had ever played. I honestly did. We played eight new songs, and I was just trying to remember what came next. I'm sure that any prayers that went out were just to remember the chords and the lyrics. The songs weren't perfect, but because we were out of the way, God could move.

We were playing a worship song called "It Is You," and there was a guy at the show who was a road manager for the Beatles and the Eagles. He had been sort of standoffish for most of the day, and he seemed like a pretty hard character. But he came into the change room and said, "I felt God. I felt something happen. I just saw..." And he was speechless. It was the first time in the whole day that he was speechless.

The thing that I loved was that he didn't really talk about the band. He didn't say, "Oh, you guys rocked," or give the old standards. I kind of got a kick out of it. I was thinking, *This is wild*, because he came in and said, "I felt God," and then he said, "I saw fathers with their hands in the air, and sons with their hands in the air, and tears coming down their faces." The worship of God's people was attractive to this guy because there is something that is really powerful about it.

After that, I just threw up my hands and thought, *Well, okay, I guess I'll just go and have bad shows the rest of my life.* But seriously, I think worship is very attractive to the outside world, more attractive than we think it is. It takes the Holy Spirit to move across a nation, which is what we've seen in the last couple of years. We have just come out of a scene in youth culture that was really about worshipping *yourself*—we had Christian mosh pits and all these crazy things going on. But we've come to a new season, and we see crowds worshipping at our shows all the time. That's not a "trend" because the one thing about true worship is that it isn't dictated by trends. It takes a humble spirit to enter into it. Worship requires people to make a sacrifice and to focus on their Creator, and it's obviously something we know He's pleased with. I've seen it firsthand.

"Knowing All the Answers"

Reaching out to others through revelation rather than argumentation brings up another area in which we misunderstand the concept of being the light. Often, because we have found Christ, who is the Truth, we think we have to have all the answers for people. We try to live as if we don't have any questions or problems of our own. This can cause us to become defensive or flustered when talking to people who simply enjoy challenging us or who have some truly difficult questions about their lives. It can also make us hide our own struggles and challenges from others—even other believers.

> We should be honest about our
> limitations and let the Holy Spirit
> reveal the truth of Christ to others.

What we sometimes forget is that it is Christ alone who is the truth. We have His truth because we have received Him and He lives in us, but we are not omniscient. The best thing we can do is to be honest about our limitations and pray that the Holy Spirit will reveal the truth of Christ to others. Ultimately, He is our Answer, for He is our salvation and life. There are simply some questions we will never be able to answer while we live on this earth.

Jody and Jeff explain how they have come to realize they don't have to "know" everything to be authentic Christians.

I feel that we put a little too much pressure on ourselves to perform, spiritually and ministry-wise. I've often felt pressured to have all the answers. One of the greatest revelations I have received in these last few years has been realizing that I don't know everything. You just don't have to have an answer for everything. I think we're sort of pressured to have an answer for everything because we're Christians and we love God and God speaks to us and we pray, so we should have an answer for everything. I would encourage anyone to think about that a little bit. I know for me it has been so much more honest just to say to people, when they ask certain questions, "You know what, I really just don't know. I'll try to find out. I'll pray about it and I'll seek counsel or I'll look into it, but for now, I don't know. It takes a lot of pressure off us to know that God's grace and His love for us is so huge that we don't have to know everything to please God. Of course, we should seek God and learn as much as we can about Him, but nobody is going to know it *all*. Sometimes we just don't know the answers, and that's okay.

I think we all have to be realistic about our shortcomings and our failures and our fallen state. I think there's nothing worse than when you meet a Christian who's "got it all figured out." When I meet someone like this, instantly, warning signals go off in my head. This is because, the more I learn about Jesus, the more questions I have.

When I was growing up, I was always told that if I had doubts about certain things, then something must be wrong with me. People would say, "How could you have doubts about Jesus? How could you question that?" I was taught not to have questions, not to wonder about anything, and not to have doubts. But the more I study about Jesus, and the more I learn about Him, the more I have to investigate things and meditate on His Word and ask questions. People sometimes think I've got all the answers, or I have it all figured out because I'm "Jeff from the Newsboys." That couldn't be further from the truth. I know that my abilities are in music, and that's what I do. That is what God has me doing. I can speak only from my experience, so that's what I try to do. I think it might do us as Christians a lot of good in reaching the world if we went on television and said, "We don't have it all figured out; we don't have all the answers, but we want to serve and help."

I think people put a lot expectations on Christian leaders to be perfect, but grace gives us the ability to be honest and real. Most Christians find that a little scary. It's hard to be open about our struggles. Being a little more vulnerable is something we have to work at every day. It's so easy to hide things, to pretend as if we've got it together. I know, because I've done it! It's hard to go to your Bible study group and say, "Look, I've got a problem with this or that." That's the hard road, but it is the best road, because it leads to grace. When you do become more open, people might look at you as if you're crazy, but grace gives you the ability to try again and to become more like Christ. We don't have to be self-righteous. Our faith is much more authentic when we are open and honest and real, and when we admit our struggles.

Make Them Wonder What You've Got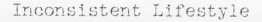

Inconsistent Lifestyle

> Before we will ever influence the heart of a
> generation, we must first earn the right to be
> heard. This is why the lifestyle of believers is so
> important: People are watching us to see how
> we handle our resources and responsibilities. They
> connect our beliefs with our actions.
> —Terry Crist

Connecting Our Beliefs with Our Actions

Another area that blocks Christ's life from shining through us is when there isn't any substance behind our witness. For example, suppose you are a young guy who wants to become a pastor, so you're working your way through school. You get a job at McDonald's. People know you are a Christian and that you want to go to seminary, but they notice that you don't put much into your job. You often leave early, and you don't carry your own weight. This causes people to think, "Christians are lazy. I don't want to have anything to do with their faith," or "Christians think they're better than others and don't have to do as much work."

There is a T-shirt that says something to the effect of, "There are 1.7 billion non-Christians in the world: Will you go and tell them?" Although that is absolutely true, sometimes we forget our own need right here: There are about 200 million people in America who really don't know what it means to be a follower of Christ. Will you go and *show* them?

This may be a cliché, but it is true: Actions speak louder than words. The key is letting Christ live His life through us so that we have the same integrity that He had. There was complete consistency in what Jesus said and what He did.

There are about 200 million
people in America who don't
really know what it means to
be a follower of Christ. Will
you go and show them?

Duncan and Jody share their thoughts about shining the light of Christ through their actions rather than just their words.

This is what shining means to me: When I go into Home Depot to buy something for my house, and I go through the checkout, I want that cashier to say, as I'm walking away, "My goodness, what has that guy got? I want that."

Shining is how we treat people. I'm someone who deals with road rage. If someone cuts me off, I think, *How dare they pull in front of me!* But if I am to shine, if I am to be an example, I can't act like a jerk. Keeping my cool is a real challenge. I'm not saying it's easy, but it's a part of my faith. You have times when you don't feel like you're very "shiny" at all. But I know there's a Scripture that says, "Do not let the sun go down on your wrath." That is especially important to practice with the people who are closest to you.

But to me, shining goes even deeper than what I've mentioned so far. It applies to our own relationship with Christ. Lately, I have been convicted to pray every day. I haven't done that routinely since becoming a Christian. But I know on the days when I do pray, I shine better than on the days when I don't get a chance to.

When you're in a band and in the kind of position we're in, it's easy to be a Christian on stage for an hour and a half. It's easy to be doing this thing that we do but, to me, the real ministry, so to speak, is in our everyday relationships; that's where the rubber meets the road—in those daily relationships and with the people we are in contact with every moment.

There have been certain situations of helping people whom I have felt God has brought along my path and which have been a real blessing to me. One time we had arrived at the city where we were going to do a show, and I was walking out to the bus behind the venue. I hadn't been up for very long, and I was feeling all crusty. But that's when I noticed a lady driving down the road with a flat tire. She pulled off to the side of the road near where I was. I was thinking to myself, *This lady isn't going to be able to change that tire.* So I ran out there and just changed her tire for her, real quick. I could tell that she didn't know where I came from, and she wasn't sure what I was doing. She was kind of uncomfortable, I think, because some guy just shows up and changes

the tire and then says, "I'll see you," and takes off. To me, those are the types of things, as small and as silly as they might seem, that help people who actually need something. You don't have to know someone to help him. You run into these situations and meet the need, and you don't receive anything in return. You just meet the person's need and then you're off. It's a simple, kind of silly thing, but it was such a blessing to *me* to be able to do that—to be able to seize that little opportunity to help someone.

Practical Ways to Show the Compassion of Christ

Let's talk now about some problems and issues in our contemporary society through which we have an opportunity to show the love of Christ to others in practical ways. People have not changed much over the centuries; when Jesus was teaching the multitudes who had gathered to hear Him, He called them "harassed and helpless, like sheep without a shepherd."

Our culture today is filled with people who are harassed—exhausted and worried about the issues they have to deal with in their lives. Christ told us that He has given us a peace that is unlike anything the world knows. It is the peace of knowing that God is always with us and that our heavenly Father is concerned about the problems and needs of our lives. We can extend this peace to others by helping to alleviate their burdens and by showing them that they are not alone in their suffering and pain.

Broken Families

We wrote a song a few years back called "Always," about growing up without a father or mother, and that really struck a chord with people. We wrote it because a friend of ours had left his wife at the time—they're back together now, but, at the time, it seemed pretty final. He seemed to have a momentary lapse of reason that caused him to leave. We knew their little girl, and so the situation hit pretty close to home. We wrote the song very quickly, but we hadn't planned on including it on the album we were working on.

We didn't realize it would touch the hearts of so many people. Every time we'd sing it at a concert, *hundreds* of people would come up and tell us how much they appreciated the song. We had never had that many people respond so strongly to a song before.

The real role models we need in our world right now are fathers and mothers who are committed to their spouses and families. A lot of youth group leaders ask us, "What do I do to keep things interesting for my kids?" or "What do I do to challenge my kids?" or "What do I do to get my kids walking on for Jesus?" The biggest thing they can do is be an example of love and trustworthiness for kids who don't have fathers and mothers whom they feel they can depend on.

The most important thing is to love these kids unconditionally, as we have been loved by Christ. We have to show grace in the same way grace has been given to us. If kids aren't experiencing the love and grace of God at home, we may be the only ones in their lives from whom they can receive it.

> We have to show grace in
> the same way grace has
> been given to us.

Simple Acts of Kindness for Those Who Are Hurting

Ultimately, the small acts of kindness are what make a significant difference in the lives of people who are going through suffering and pain. The story of Jody's daughter that we included at the beginning of this book has much more to it that we want to share with you now. It demonstrates how helping others in their suffering by meeting their practical, everyday needs is a powerful way we can shine the light of Christ.

Peter describes how the actions of the members of Jody's church helped him understand more about how to serve others during difficult times, and then Jody explains how much he and his family were encouraged and strengthened by their loving church community.

Within thirty minutes after Bethany was brought to the hospital, there were all these people gathered at the hospital, and I didn't know who half of them were. Jody introduced them to me, and they were all from his church. I saw a whole community come together to help one of their families. I wasn't used to seeing that happen. When people hear that you or a family member are in the hospital, you often get flowers or a box of chocolates or something, but people don't usually camp out near your bedside. These people came to show their support, and they stayed. When it first happened, they were there for two weeks. They just slept there at the hospital on the couches or whatever they could find to sleep on. Every time we went to visit Jody and his family, people were everywhere.

What happened to Bethany was a very tragic thing, but God has used her already in so many great ways and in so many people's lives. It's just amazing. It blows us away. Even the work that God has done with us, with our family and in the band, because of the whole ordeal has been amazing. She's been such an incredible blessing to others.

It was really great to feel all our Christian brothers and sisters around us during that time. It started, of course, with everyone in the band and their families, and then our families and the members of the church that Erica and I go to. We had really great support from there. And then all the prayer support that went out—probably half of the churches in Nashville! We would hear all the time of all the different churches and people who were praying for Bethany. Every day, we would hear of more places, even in Europe, because we've established relationships with people over there from our tours. There were churches in France and England that were praying for Bethany. It made you feel the international church community, that it was a *real* community in that way, and it was really a neat thing to feel.

It's been just amazing to hear of all the great things that have come out of this whole situation. For example, one of the nurses who didn't actually have Bethany as a patient, but who knew that Bethany was in the hospital because she was a friend of Erica's, would come over to intensive care and visit Bethany when she had her shift at the hospital. She told us, "Man, this whole situation has changed people around here. This is really turning this place upside down." She didn't really go into details, but we knew what she meant. Usually, in that type of situation, everything becomes so clinical for the doctors and nurses. I think it almost has to. For them to be emotionally involved with every patient would be too difficult because people's circumstances are so hard and so tragic. But I think Bethany's case was something that kind of broke through that for a lot of them, especially her coming through this illness that no other child had ever survived. They saw all the support we had from our friends and our church. They also saw how Erica and I were there to support and encourage Bethany.

When you are a parent, and you go into a situation like that, you're scared of everything. You see your child with all these tubes and all the IV's and everything else, and you're very worried about her. I think that babies know how people around them are feeling. So we tried to just be very loving and encouraging the whole time. The fact that we were able to do that was a gift from God. He helped us not to worry, but just to love her.

You can't be in intensive care for twenty-four hours a day because of doctors' rounds and all these different things. Also, there were many kids in IC together, and if something starts going bad with one kid, everybody has to leave. But any time we could, we made sure we were there, and we tried to encourage Bethany the whole time. We wanted to be there as much as possible to communicate with her, touch her, and hold her. Just anything we could do. I think that was something that was maybe a little different from what the hospital staff had seen a lot of.

People also did little things that really made a difference to us emotionally. After about two or three days of being at the hospital, I realized I hadn't really eaten during all that time. There was a group from a church who had come to the hospital with soup and bread and cookies and things like that. They served it in one little area on that floor. Anybody who had a child in intensive care or on that floor was welcome to come and have a bowl of soup. Since

I hadn't eaten in a couple of days, I remember literally crying over this bowl of soup because although it was small, it was exactly what I needed.

I'd really like to encourage people to get involved in doing little things like that. When we are young, we have these grandiose dreams of doing things to serve God, but I think there's so much that can be done that is simple. Simple little things like that, but which make such a difference in people's lives. Erica and I have talked about some things since that time that we want to do. We would like to go back to the hospital and do for others what people did for us. I remember getting a packet of stuff like toiletries—toothbrushes and deodorant and things like that. It was just something that somebody from our church had taken the time to put together and bring down to the hospital so that it was there for people who were in our position. It was a great thing. Things like that are seemingly small, but they are things that all of us can do. To me, that's what shining really is.

Make Them Wonder What You've Got

When There Are No Words

Sometimes, when people are going through extremely difficult times, the best thing we can do is simply express our love for them. Phil describes how his friendship with a young boy has taught him this vital truth.

Recently, I got a call from a kid I've been in touch with for about four years. He's really, really sick, and I've visited him a few times. He saw me once and asked, "Will you come down and play for my youth group?" I said yes and went. He wasn't expected to live beyond the age of eight, and I think he's heading toward the end now.

When he called me, I didn't know what to say, but it didn't matter. All that mattered was that I was there with him on the phone, and we hung out and talked. He could barely speak, and I didn't have much to say. I didn't want to talk about the new Play Station games or anything like that. I was just there. He heard me crying. I heard his pain, and I told him I loved him. That's as much as can be delivered over the phone.

More powerful than words, though, are actions. I'm going to see him soon, and I'm just going to hang out with him and love him. That's what needs to happen, I think. Words are words, and they do have the power to heal, *but hugs are better.*

I'm learning that, and so I find myself hugging people a whole lot more now. When I meet people who are in need, I just hang on to them; I don't want to let them go. I cry with them. I think there's something healing as we share one another's burdens. I don't know what it is. It's probably some sort of deep theological, biblical principle. But it's what the Lord wants me to do so many times when I come across people who are desperately in need. I just want to love them and hug them and not let them go. Sometimes I wish I had super words of wisdom to tell them, but I'm really trying to make a point of listening to what the Holy Spirit is saying to me.

In most situations, more often than not, it's an action—a physical action—that's required. Usually a hug or a smile or a caress is what's really important. We need to be people of love. At the same time, we need to be firm and strong, realizing that there is evil and wrong in this world. We need to be gentle as lambs and as ferocious as lions. We are the Lord's ambassadors. The Lord tells us concerning people in need, "Love them. Soothe them. Feed them. Care for the widows, give to the poor, feed the hungry." So much of it involves actions.

Responding to Pain and Suffering throughout the World

Involvement in Service and Missions Overseas

A very positive movement we're seeing today is the increasing involvement of young people in service and missions overseas. Jeff describes how encouraged he is by this development and the impact it has made on his own family.

I'm really excited about what I'm seeing, because I look at groups like Teen Mania who were just starting out ten years ago, taking a few hundred people on these missions trips that they do every summer. And now, it's like every kid's going on a mission trip every summer, every kid's raising money, and I think a lot of that is starting to make a difference. It seems like there's a whole new movement going on where the youth generation is really being encouraged to serve others, which I think is commendable considering the fact that in our culture, there are so many things pulling for our attention every minute of the day.

It seems like everyone's telling you what you need all the time. There are ads all over the place here, such as

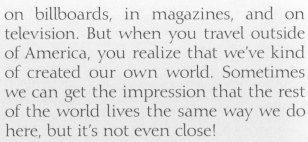

on billboards, in magazines, and on television. But when you travel outside of America, you realize that we've kind of created our own world. Sometimes we can get the impression that the rest of the world lives the same way we do here, but it's not even close!

Even though there are many distractions, I think a lot of kids are finally getting fed up with it. It is as if they are saying, "Enough! Let's just put this aside, get out of this country, and go somewhere and *help* people." I know that traveling outside the United States and seeing the needs of people overseas has been a big awakening for me. I had never really traveled outside of the city I grew up in, Detroit, until I was nineteen years old and joined the band. It seems as if I've seen the whole world in the last ten years.

There are just so many hurting people out there. It's incredible what we have here. There are many times when I've gone places to help people, and it's changed *me* much more than the people I went to help. That is why, every time I see a kid getting involved in service, I say, "Yes! That's so cool," because they will never be the same again. Whether they go to a third-world country, a nursing home, or inner city, the Gospel will then become real. That's when the meaning of the Gospel really hits home. My sister, who is twenty-six years old now, went on a mission trip when she was fifteen. She works in an office now and is pretty integrated into society. But I know that, even to this day, there's a part of her that still has a burden in her heart for people overseas because she was able to break out of the mind-set of our society where we just aren't allowed a minute to think about the needs of others.

So it's a two-sided thing. We help others, and we gain a blessing in return. It's a powerful thing. I think this movement to help people overseas is spreading quickly, from what I've seen. If you want to talk about positive changes that are reflecting Christ's life, that's a massive one.

It's exciting to me that people are starting to grasp this concept of serving others, because that's what Jesus did. He came to serve.

Shine

Involvement in Critical Issues

Finally, we want to talk about some of the critical issues facing our world today—issues that are really life and death for the people involved. Jesus said, "I was hungry and you gave me something to eat, I was thirsty and you gave me something to drink, I was a stranger and you invited me in, I needed clothes and you clothed me, I was sick and you looked after me, I was in prison and you came to visit me." This call to help those in desperate need is one we need to take a close look at to see if we are truly fulfilling it in the way we should be. Although there are many complicated aspects to world problems, such as AIDS and hunger, the important thing is that we are seeking God as to what He would have us do in alleviating the real suffering of others.

Peter describes how he felt when the issue of AIDS first came to public attention. We conclude with some questions to ponder as we grapple with these crucial issues of our times.

 When AIDS hit the scene, I didn't know what to think. I'm usually someone who doesn't run to a decision too quickly, thank God. I have done this on some occasions and made mistakes, but at that time I remember distinctly saying, "What is this *really?*" Some people were stating, "This is a punishment," and other foolish things. However, it

really came to me that maybe this was a challenge for us, an opportunity, even.

There are certain times in the Word where you see God giving people an opportunity to help others in need. For as long as I can remember, I've seen us as a church make a certain response to the AIDS crisis. Some of this hasn't been working. If we've done one thing and it isn't working, perhaps we should try something different. Sometimes you find wisdom in that approach, as long as it lines up with the Scriptures. To me, our approach should always be to do unto others what we would want to have done to us, which is to provide help and healing.

Today, many have forgotten that there is a reason that, all over America, there are hospitals called St. Mark's and St. Joseph's. It is because they were started by Christians. They were founded by great Christian people, but now they are just monuments that are part of the culture. People don't remember the motivations of those who started them. This is a challenge to us today to figure out what has been working and what hasn't been working, and to follow the example of those earlier Christians who cared about those who were suffering and who translated their concern into practical action.

What If?

What if, when people heard the word *Christian*, they didn't think "hypocritical," "judgmental," or "self-righteous," but instead thought "loving," "peaceful," and "full of a strange, unspeakable joy"?

What if, when people heard the word *Christian*, they said, "They're the people who fought the fight against AIDS. They're the people who are making major strides to eliminate poverty in Africa"?

What if, when people heard the word *Christian*, they said, "They're the ones who act as if they've been forgiven a debt they couldn't pay"?

As we seek to serve and love as Christ did, we will be visited by God's mercy and grace, and the land of shadow will be transformed by the radiance of His light.

I must keep alive in myself
the desire for my true country,
which I shall not find till
after death; I must never let
it get snowed under or turned
aside; I must make it the main
object of life to press on to
that other country and to help
others to do the same.

—C. S. Lewis

Part VI

Appetite for Eternity

Since, then, you have been raised with Christ, set your hearts on things above, where Christ is seated at the right hand of God. Set your minds on things above, not on earthly things. For you died, and your life is now hidden with Christ in God.

—Colossians 3:1-3

Lord, I don't know where all this is going
Or how it all works out
Lead me to peace that is past understanding
A peace beyond all doubt

You are the God of tomorrow
Turning the darkness to dawn
Lifting the hopeless with hope to go on
You are the rock of all salvation

"Lord (I Don't Know)"
Thrive

We know also that the Son of God has come and has given us understanding, so that we may know him who is true. And we are in him who is true—even in his Son Jesus Christ. He is the true God and eternal life.

–1 John 5:20

If we consider the unblushing promises of reward and the staggering nature of the rewards promised in the Gospels, it would seem that Our Lord finds our desires not too strong, but too weak. We are half-hearted creatures...when infinite joy is offered us....We are far too easily pleased.

—C. S. Lewis

You've heard the question, "What would you do differently if you knew you had only a few days left to live?"

Yet the ultimate question is this: "What would you do differently if you knew that you would live forever, that whatever you did today would affect you for the rest of that eternal life?"

While the first question is hypothetical, the second one isn't. We *are* eternal beings, and we *are* going to live forever.

Earthly life has eternal ramifications. The choices and decisions that we make now will influence the future, not only for ourselves, but also for others. Are we living the lives we would be proud to present to God at the end of time? Are our values and priorities toward other people the same as Christ's, so that He will say to us, "Whatever you did for one of the least of these brothers of mine, you did for me"?

God has given us many good things to enjoy here on earth. But, as we have seen, this life also has many distractions, secondary priorities, worries, and temptations that would pull us away from the priority of the eternal. We have a very real enemy who tries to keep us from setting our minds on things above our earthly existence. These things divert our focus to what is only temporary and ultimately unsatisfying so that we forget about storing treasures where they cannot rust—heaven. This is why Jesus kept emphasizing so strongly that when we seek to gain our own lives, we will lose them, but that eternity awaits those who surrender their lives for Christ's sake. "The man who loves his life will lose it, while the man who hates his life in this world will keep it *for eternal life.*"

God asks us,

Why spend money on what is not bread, and your labor on what does not satisfy? Listen, listen to me, and eat what is good, and your soul will delight in the richest of fare.

Jesus echoed this very thought when He said,

Do not work for food that spoils, but for food that endures to eternal life, which the Son of Man will give you. On him God the Father has placed his seal of approval.

The only thing that will ultimately satisfy us is Jesus Himself. He is the Bread of Life. To know Him is to know eternal life: "Now this is eternal life: that they may know you, the only true God, and Jesus Christ, whom you have sent."

How do we keep this life in perspective with eternal realities? The only way is to have an *appetite for eternity*.

This is what Paul meant by setting our hearts and minds on things above, where Christ is. When we receive Christ, He dwells in us, and our lives are "hidden" in Him. There is a complete blending of our lives. Although this happens at salvation, we have seen that this is also a continuous process. The more we lose ourselves, the more our lives are hidden in Him so that the only thing others see is His light and life shining through us. This is how we can "be the change we want to see." This is how the world will be transformed.

We can ask our heavenly Father each day to give us this appetite for eternity, so that our minds and hearts are always joined to His. It should be our continual prayer. An appetite for eternity will

- ☀ Inspire us to make the most of our lives.

- ☀ Help us to put this life in perspective.

- ☀ Help us understand the true nature of eternal life.

- ☀ Enable us to view others in the light of eternity.

- ☀ Allow us to keep our focus on the Eternal One.

Shine

Make the Most of Your Life

Our challenge is to make the most of our lives here so that they will count for eternity. We must use them for what is lasting, not temporary. An appetite for eternity will help us always to keep in mind eternal realities and eternal potential. We don't want to focus on the wrong things and then realize too late what is really important in life. Regret over the way we have lived our lives will be kept to a minimum when we maintain an appetite for eternity.

Put This Life in Perspective

When we rest the whole weight of our lives on what is eternal, we can trust God to take care of us in this world. It is in the light of the eternal that we can gain a better perspective of the worries and cares of tomorrow. Here we see our reliance on God for our daily bread and for our eternal future come together. No matter where we are or what happens to us in life, He has said, "I will never leave you nor forsake you." Remember that "Jesus Christ is the same yesterday, today, and forever."

Understand the True Nature of Eternal Life

Sometimes, as we live our busy lives, we can get the impression that heaven is "out there" and far away. But we can't let this idea influence our perspective of eternal life.

As C. S. Lewis said in *Christian Reflections,* "Where except in the present can the eternal be met?"

Our eternal life in Christ began the moment we asked Him to come into our lives. This means that eternity is not so much a *place* as it is a *position,* a position of being in the immediate presence of God. When we were given the gift of the Holy Spirit, we entered into that presence—or rather, that presence entered into us. It is God who makes heaven a paradise, and any place without Him is simply hell.

"The kingdom of God is within you" means that our eternal life is here and now. "Now we see but a poor reflection as in a mirror," but one day the picture will be made stunningly clear to us. Then we will see the Eternal One face to face. Yet eternity is not some distant goal. We are already living in it.

View Others in the Light of Eternity

Jesus made it very clear that the way we treat people on this earth has eternal ramifications—not only for them, but also for us. We owe every person respect because we are dealing with eternal beings made in God's image. Everyone we meet has an eternal future—either with God or without Him.

When we truly shine the light of Christ, we will make people wonder because, every person, Christian or otherwise, carries within himself a longing for the eternal,

although he usually does not recognize it for what it is. Only through the revelation of God can people see what this longing really is—a longing for the Eternal One. Shining the light of Christ can awaken the spark of the eternal in others.

Perhaps you recognize that spark within yourself, but feel you have never fully come into the light of Christ. Christ died so that we may have life, that those who believe in Him by faith shall receive salvation and truly see the light of eternity, which is only in Him. The only way you can have an appetite for eternity is if you have first tasted it. If you have never received Christ into your life, we invite you now to accept that He died on the cross to pay the price for your sin and to surrender your life to Him so that you can truly enter into eternal life. Christ is the Way to the Father, and He stands at the door of your heart waiting to be asked in.

Keep Your Focus on the Eternal One

We all must keep alive in ourselves an appetite for eternity. To shine is to press on to that "other country," as Lewis said, and to "help others to do the same." We do this by fixing our eyes on Jesus, the light and the life of all men.

> For our light and momentary troubles are achieving for us an eternal glory that far outweighs them all. So we fix our eyes not on what is seen, but on what is unseen. For what is seen is temporary, but what is unseen is eternal.

Turn your eyes upon Jesus
Look full in his wonderful face
And the things of earth will grow strangely dim
In the light of his glory and grace

"Where You Belong/Turn Your Eyes upon Jesus"
Shine: The Hits

Part I

What obstacles in your life keep
Christ's light from shining on you or
out to others?

If you are the only Christ some people
see, what will they know about Him
because of you?

How can you let your light shine
today—starting with your family, then
moving out into your world? What will
it mean for you to "Be the change you
want to see"?

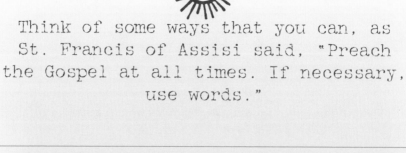

Think of some ways that you can, as St. Francis of Assisi said, "Preach the Gospel at all times. If necessary, use words."

Part II

How can you avoid conforming to the world's view of success?

What will it take for you to go
through the eye of the needle and leave
yourself behind?

The Beatitudes (Matthew 5:3-12)
epitomize the principles of the
upside-down kingdom. How is God
helping you to live out these
teachings in your everyday life?

_____

_____

_____

_____

_____

_____

_____

_____

_____

_____

_____

_____

_____

_____

_____

_____

_____

_____

_____

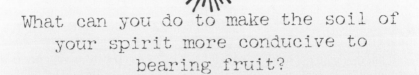

What can you do to make the soil of
your spirit more conducive to
bearing fruit?

_____

_____

_____

_____

_____

_____

_____

_____

_____

_____

_____

_____

_____

_____

_____

_____

_____

_____

_____

_____

_____

_____

Part III

Have you experienced the richness of solitude with God? How has this affected your Christian walk?

_____

_____

_____

_____

_____

_____

_____

_____

_____

_____

_____

_____

_____

_____

_____

_____

_____

_____

_____

_____

_____

_____

Do you feel accepted by God? What can
you do to open your heart and believe
that He loves you just because He
created you?

What kind of devotional habits have you tried to maintain? Is your system working for you? If not, what can you do to discover the kind of relationship God wants to have with you? Do you have a Sabbath in your week? What steps can you take to apply this principle in your life?

_____

_____

_____

_____

_____

_____

_____

_____

_____

_____

_____

_____

_____

_____

_____

_____

_____

Look back at the past few years of your life. What moments have defined the person God wants you to be and where He wants to take you? Can you see how He was working in ways you didn't understand at the time?

Part IV

Dying to yourself means sometimes giving up your rights. How does surrendering yourself "as unto the Lord" change your perspective on this?

_____

_____

_____

_____

_____

_____

_____

_____

_____

_____

_____

_____

_____

_____

_____

_____

_____

_____

_____

_____

Is there imbalance in your life of service? Do you serve when it is easy (like giving change to a homeless person) but not when it is hard (when a family member wants your help—again)? How can you know whether you are truly serving "as unto the Lord"?

Have you experienced the joy that comes from true surrender, or have you settled for the shallow happiness that comes from promoting yourself?

Do you have a place in a strong
Christian community? What can you do
to connect with the body of Christ
around you?

Are there reasons that you haven't opened yourself to relationships with other Christians? Are these reasons truly valid? What can you do to follow God through the healing and reconnecting process?

_____

_____

_____

_____

_____

_____

_____

_____

_____

_____

_____

_____

_____

_____

_____

_____

_____

_____

Part V

When you see people making sinful choices, which comes more naturally to you—judgment or compassion?

Do you assume that people won't want to talk to you or get to know you? Do you assume that you have nothing to say? God has called you to be involved in the world around you: What can you do to face this truth?

_____

_____

_____

_____

_____

_____

_____

_____

_____

_____

_____

_____

_____

_____

_____

_____

_____

_____

_____

_____

Are you comfortable with the idea that you don't have an answer for every question? Do you feel pressure to have everything at your fingertips? Or do you tend to be prideful because you feel as though you do have the answers?

How often do you see life's little opportunites to shine? Do you tend to look past them, toward grandiose ideas of "serving God"? What can you do to make sure that you don't miss the critical moments that make a true difference?

What areas of your life or witness just haven't been "working"? How would Jesus turn your habits around? Would He do the opposite of what you've been doing? What can you do to be as real as He was?

Part VI

Setting your mind on eternity will, in a kind of paradox, help you to view today without being stressed about tomorrow. What can you do to focus on the important things in life, instead of merely on the urgent ones?

_____

_____

_____

_____

_____

_____

_____

_____

_____

_____

_____

_____

_____

_____

_____

_____

_____

_____

_____

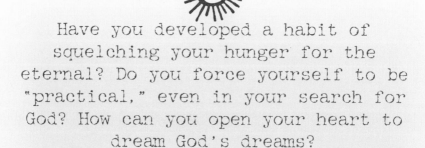

Have you developed a habit of
squelching your hunger for the
eternal? Do you force yourself to be
"practical," even in your search for
God? How can you open your heart to
dream God's dreams?

Even while gazing at the most beautiful Person in the universe, we can
be distracted from God's presence and
blessing. What things most easily draw
you away? What can you do to "turn your
eyes upon Jesus"?

_____
_____
_____
_____
_____
_____
_____
_____
_____
_____
_____
_____
_____
_____
_____
_____
_____
_____
_____
_____
_____

It is God's presence that makes heaven
what it is, and His absence that makes
a hell. Which position better describes
your life? What can you do to invite
Him to manifest His presence in your
daily life?

_____

_____

_____

_____

_____

_____

_____

_____

_____

_____

_____

_____

_____

_____

_____

_____

_____

_____

You've heard the question, "What would you do differently if you knew you had only a few days left to live?" Now, ask yourself this: "What would I do differently if I knew that I would live forever, and that whatever I did today would affect me for the rest of my eternal life?"

_____

_____

_____

_____

_____

_____

_____

_____

_____

_____

_____

_____

_____

_____

_____

_____

_____

_____

Books of Influence

Buchanan, Mark. *Your God Is Too Safe: Rediscovering the Wonder of a God You Can't Control.* Sisters, OR: Multnomah, 2001.

Buechner, Frederick. *The Sacred Journey.* New York: HarperCollins, 1982.

——. *The Alphabet of Grace.* New York: HarperCollins, 1989.

——. *Whistling in the Dark.* New York: HarperCollins, 1993.

Chesterton, G. K. *Orthodoxy.* 1908. Reprint, San Francisco: Ignatius Press, 1995.

——. *The Everlasting Man.* 1925. Reprint, San Francisco: Ignatius Press, 1993.

Crist, Terry M. *Learning the Language of Babylon: Changing the World by Engaging the Culture.* Grand Rapids: Chosen Books, Baker Book House, 2001.

Dostoevsky, Fyodor. *Notes from Underground.* 1863. Norton Critical Edition, Edited by Michael R. Katz. New York: W. W. Norton, 2000.

Evrist, Dale. *The Mighty Hand of God.* Lake Mary, FL: Creation House, 2000.

Green, Melody, and David Hazard. *No Compromise: The Life Story of Keith Green.* Eugene, OR: Harvest House Publishers, 2000.

Lewis, C. S. *God in the Dock.* 1970. Reprint, Grand Rapids: Williams B. Eerdmans Publishing Company, 1997.

——. *The Great Divorce.* New York: HarperCollins, 2001.

——. *Mere Christianity.* New York: HarperCollins, 2001.

——. *The Screwtape Letters.* New York: HarperCollins, 2001.

——. *The Weight of Glory.* New York: HarperCollins, 2001.

Manning, Brennan. *Abba's Child: The Cry of the Heart for Intimate Belonging.* Colorado Springs, NavPress, 1994.

———. *The Signature of Jesus.* Sisters, OR: Multnomah, 1996.

———. *The Ragamuffin Gospel.* Sisters, OR: Multnomah, 2000.

———. *Ruthless Trust: The Ragamuffin's Path to God.* New York: HarperCollins, 2000.

Merton, Thomas. *The Seven Storey Mountain.* 1948. Fiftieth Anniversary Edition, New York: Harcourt Brace & Company, 1998.

Nair, Ken. *Discovering the Mind of a Woman.* Nashville: Thomas Nelson, 1995.

Tolstoy, Leo. *Walk in the Light & Twenty-three Tales.* 1928. Reprint, Farmington, PA: Plough Publishing House, The Bruderhof Foundation, 1998.

Tozer, A. W. *Renewed Day by Day.* Compiled by G. B. Smith. Camp Hill, PA: Christian Publications, 1980.

Wilkinson, Bruce H. *Secrets of the Vine: Breaking Through to Abundance.* Sisters, OR: Multnomah, 2001.

Yancey, Philip. *The Jesus I Never Knew.* Grand Rapids: Zondervan, 1995.

———. *What's So Amazing About Grace?* Grand Rapids: Zondervan, 1997.

———. *The Bible Jesus Read.* Grand Rapids: Zondervan, HarperCollins, 1999.

———. *Reaching for the Invisible God: What Can We Expect to Find?* Grand Rapids: Zondervan, HarperCollins, 2000.

———. *Soul Survivor: How My Faith Survived the Church.* New York: Doubleday, 2001.

Sources

Prelude

14: *"Think of these"*: Frederick Buechner. *The Alphabet of Grace* (New York: HarperCollins, 1982), p. vii.

Part One

17: *"And the end"*: T. S. Eliot. Qtd. in Philip Yancey's, *Soul Survivor: How My Faith Survived the Church* (New York: Doubleday, 2001), p. 59.

21: *"Down here in the valley"*: "Thrive." Peter Furler/Steve Taylor. © 2002. Ariose Music/ASCAP. All rights administered by EMI Christian Music Publishing. Used by permission.

23: *"The gospel will persuade"*: Brennan Manning. *The Signature of Jesus* (Sisters, OR: Multnomah, 1996), p. 17.

25: *"seek first the kingdom"*: Matthew 6:33 NKJV.

26: *"Come to me"*: Matthew 11:28.

26: *"A new command"*: John 13:34.

26: *"God did not send"*: John 3:17.

27: *"The Word became flesh"*: John 1:14.

28: *"the light of the world"*: John 8:12; 9:5.

28: *"You are the light"*: Matthew 5:14.

28: *"Let your light"*: Matthew 5:16.

32: *"You are the salt"*: Matthew 5:13–16.

33: *"If then the light"*: Matthew 6:23.

33: *"When Jesus told"*: See Matthew 13:33; Luke 13:21 for the parable of the yeast.

33: *"preserve the culture"*: See Matthew 5:13; Mark 9:50; Luke 14:34.

35: *"a holy nation"*: See 1 Peter 2:9.

37: *"Jesus told of the man"*: See Matthew 18:23–35.

39: *"God is not willing"*: See 2 Peter 3:9 NKJV.

40: *"By this all men"*: John 13:35.

41: *"in the world"*: See John 17:14–16, 18.

41: *"Jesus was the friend"*: See Matthew 9:10; 11:19; Luke 7:34.

41: *"The man without the Spirit"*: 1 Corinthians 2:14.

42: *"How did we go":* Terry M. Crist. *Learning the Language of Babylon: Changing the World by Engaging the Culture* (Grand Rapids: Baker Books, 2001), p. 14.

43: *"the fragmentation":* The Penguin Dictionary of Philosophy, s.v. "postmodernism."

44: *"die to ourselves":* Galatians 2:20.

45: *"take up our cross":* Luke 9:23.

46: *"In him was life":* John 1:4.

46: *"For as the Father":* John 5:26.

48: *"Lead me to the rock":* Psalm 61:2.

48: *"Why do you call":* Luke 6:46–49.

48: *"The man who walks":* John 12:35–36.

49: *"there is no one righteous":* Romans 3:10.

50: *"Be the change":* See Philip Yancey. *Soul Survivor: How My Faith Survived the Church* (New York: Doubleday, 2001), p. 172. Mahatma Ghandi said, "We must become the change we want to see." We've taken that thought and put it into a more active form: "Be the change you want to see." Although Ghandi lived out many of the truths Christ taught, sadly, he never came to know Him as his personal Savior. Philip Yancey writes, "Throughout his life, Gandhi found himself going back to the teachings of Jesus....Still, he could not reconcile the disparity he saw between Christ and Christians." Perhaps if Ghandi had encountered more Christians whose lives had been radically transformed through surrender to Christ, so that His light had been clearly seen in them, it would have made a difference. We never know who is watching our lives, and the difference our faithfulness to Christ could mean for the kingdom of God.

50: *"take the log out":* See Matthew 7:3–5.

50: *"Do to others":* Luke 6:31.

51: *"The people walking":* Isaiah 9:2–3.

Part Two

53: *"Shine: make em wonder":* "Shine." Peter Furler/Steve Taylor. © 1994 Ariose Music/ASCAP. All rights administered by EMI Christian Music Publishing.

55: *"Nothing is wonderful":* C. S. Lewis. *God in the Dock* (1970, reprint, Grand Rapids: William B. Eerdmans, 1997), p. 26.

59: *"And every generation":* "Cornelius." Peter Furler/Steve Taylor. © 2002 Ariose Music/ASCAP. All rights administered by EMI Christian Publishing. Used by permission.

66: *"a kingdom of priests":* Exodus 19:6.

67: *"The kingdom of God":* Mark 1:15.

68: *"The kingdom of heaven is like treasure":* Matthew 13:44.

68: *"Again, the kingdom":* Matthew 13:45–46.

68: *"The gospel of the kingdom":* Matthew 24:14.

69: *"Yours, O LORD, is the greatness":* 1 Chronicles 29:11.

69: *"Your kingdom come. Your will be done":* Matthew 6:10 NKJV.

69: *"For Yours is":* Matthew 6:13 NKJV.

70: *"Jesus went through":* Matthew 9:35.

70: *"the sign the kingdom":* See Matthew 11:2–5.

70: *"He gave them power":* Luke 9:1–2.

71: *"After his suffering":* Acts 1:3.

71: *"And this gospel":* Matthew 24:14.

71: *"The disciples took":* Regarding the disciples taking the kingdom message seriously, note that Philip preached the kingdom (Acts 8:12); Paul and Barnabus preached the kingdom (Acts 14:22); Paul preached the kingdom when he traveled alone (Acts 19:8; 20:25); and Paul, at the end of his life, taught daily on the principles of the kingdom of God (Acts 28:23, 31).

71: *"But seek first":* Matthew 6:33.

72: *"Do not worry":* Matthew 6:25–33.

73: *"Listen! A farmer":* Mark 4:3–8.

74: *"He who has ears":* Mark 4:9.

74: *"The secret of the kingdom":* Mark 4:11, 13.

74: *"The farmer sows":* Mark 4:14–15.

74: *"Others, like seed":* Mark 4:16–17.

75: *"Still others, like seed":* Mark 4:18–19.

75: *"Others, like seed":* Mark 4:20.

76: *"Do you bring":* Mark 4:21–23.

76: *"Jesus spoke all":* Matthew 13:34–35.

76: *"I have become"*: Colossians 1:25–27, emphasis added.

77: *"The kingdom of God"*: Luke 17:21.

77: *"No one can see"*: John 3:3, 5.

77: *"Do not be afraid"*: Luke 12:32.

77: *"good news of great joy"*: Luke 2:10, emphasis added.

77: *"everyone is pressing"*: Luke 16:16 NKJV.

78: *"yoke is easy"*: See Matthew 11:30.

78: *"I will put my laws"*: Hebrews 8:10.

79: *"Your attitude should be"*: Philippians 2:5–11.

80: *"If anyone would come"*: Matthew 16:24.

80: *"In the upside-down"*: Donald B. Kraybill, *The Upside-Down Kingdom*, rev. ed. (Scottdale, PA: Herald Press, 1990), p. 243.

80: *"The other gods"*: Excerpt from "Jesus of the Scars" by Edward Shillito (1872–1948) accessed at <http://www.christiananswers.net/q-aiia/god-pain.html> (17 June 2002).

81: *"I tell you the truth"*: Matthew 19:23–24.

81: *"I tell you the truth"*: Mark 10:15.

82: *"Whoever humbles himself"*: Matthew 18:4.

82: *"Whoever wants to save"*: Mark 8:35.

83: *"I can do all things"*: Philippians 4:13 NKJV.

84: *"old man"*: See Romans 6:6 NKJV, Ephesians 4:22 NKJV, and Colossians 3:9 NKJV.

84: *"It is easier"*: Matthew 19:24.

84: *"Submit to one another"*: Ephesians 5:21.

85: *"The kingdom of God"*: Romans 14:17–18.

85: *"ever hearing"*: Isaiah 6:9.

85: *"Repent, for the kingdom"*: Matthew 4:17, emphasis added.

86: *"There is a way"*: Proverbs 14:12.

86: *"For my thoughts"*: Isaiah 55:8–9.

86: *"Though God has made"*: Ecclesiastes 7:29 TLB.

86: *"There is but one good"*: C. S. Lewis, *The Great Divorce* (New York: HarperCollins, 2001), p. 106.

87: *"What is highly"*: Luke 16:15.

88: *"If you hold"*: John 8:31–32.

88: *"No one sews"*: Matthew 9:16–17.

89: *"Repent, then, and turn"*: Acts 3:19.

91: *"Whoever practices"*: Matthew 5:19.

93: *"When he, the Spirit"*: John 16:13.

93: *"yeast that a woman"*: Matthew 13:33.

94: *"working out our salvation"*: See Philippians 2:12.

94: *"A man had a fig tree"*: Luke 13:6–9.

95: *"The kingdom of God"*: Matthew 21:43.

95: *"that they should repent"*: Acts 26:20.

97: *"A man of noble birth"*: Luke 19:12–26.

99: *"I have been crucified"*: Galatians 2:20.

100: *"When [Jesus] saw"*: Matthew 9:36–38.

100: *"good news of great joy"*: Luke 2:10, emphasis added.

100: *"The time has come"*: Mark 1:15.

100: *"separate the sheep"*: See Matthew 25:32.

101: *"The kingdom of heaven is like"*: Matthew 13:24–30.

102: *"The truth is in"*: "Shine." Peter Furler/Steve Taylor. © 1994.
    Ariose Music/ASCAP. All rights administered by EMI Christian
    Publishing. Used by permission.

104: *"The kingdom of heaven is like"*: Matthew 13:31–32.

104: *"[Jesus] showed himself"*: Acts 1:3–8.

105: *"Whoever wants to become"*: Matthew 20:26–28.

106: *"[Jesus] said to another man"*: Luke 9:59–62.

107: *"A certain man"*: Luke 14:16–24.

108: *"There are people"*: Frederick Buechner, *Whistling in the Dark* (New
    York: HarperCollins, 1993), p. 88.

109: *"A righteous man"*: Psalm 112:6–7.

110: *"Of all the commandments"*: Mark 12:28.

111: *"Love the Lord"*: Mark 12:30–31.

112: *"Whoever finds his life"*: Matthew 10:39.

113: *"The Christian ideal"*: G. K. Chesterton, *What's Wrong with the
    World*, Chapter Five, Qtd. in Philip Yancey's, *Soul Survivor: How
    My Faith Survived the Church* (New York: Doubleday, 2001), p. 58.

122: *"If it is possible"*: Romans 12:18.

Part Three

131: *"You cannot love"*: C. S. Lewis. *The Great Divorce* (New York:
    HarperCollins, 2001), p. 100.

135: *"When you're dull"*: "Where You Belong." Peter Furler/Steve Taylor. © 1992 Ariose Music/ASCAP. All rights administered by EMI Christian Music Publishing. Used by permission.

139: *"There is only one"*: Thomas Merton. *The Seven Storey Mountain* (New York: Harcourt Brace & Company, 1948, renewed 1976. This edition is the fiftieth anniversary edition, published in 1990), p. 407.

139: *"After the earthquake"*: 1 Kings 19:12.

140: *"in the cool"*: Genesis 3:8.

140: *"For God, who said"*: 2 Corinthians 4:6.

141: *"We can make"*: Brother Lawrence. *The Practice of the Presence of God* (New Kensington, PA: Whitaker House, 1982), 33.

142: *"These people come"*: Isaiah 29:13.

143: *"I will give"*: Ezekiel 11:19–20.

144: *"It is God"*: Philippians 2:13.

145: *"Her many sins"*: Luke 7:47, emphasis added.

145: *"Your faith has saved"*: Luke 7:50.

145: *"Do you love"*: John 21:17.

145: *"Yes, Lord, you know"*: John 21:16.

145: *"Feed my sheep"*: John 21:17.

145: *"Above all, love"*: 1 Peter 4:8.

148: *"There was a man"*: Luke 15:11–24.

150: *"My Lord, God"*: Thomas Merton. *Thoughts in Solitude* (New York: Farrar, Straus & Cudahy, 1958), p. 83.

151: *"Trust represents"*: Philip Yancey. *Soul Survivor: How My Faith Survived the Church* (New York: Doubleday, 2001), p. 214.

152: *"practicing the presence"*: Brother Lawrence. *The Practice of the Presence....* This concept is discussed throughout the book.

152: *"engagement of the heart"*: Jonathan Edwards, qtd. in *Devotional Classics*, eds. Richard J. Foster and James Bryan Smith (New York: HarperCollins, 1993), p. 19.

152: *"holy affection"*: Ibid., p. 19.

152: *"spiritual agility"*: Ibid., p. 27.

152: *"spiritual exercises"*: Ibid., p. 36.

152: *"becoming God's friend"*: Ibid., p. 157.

152: *"To be with Him"*: Brother Lawrence. *The Practice of the Presence...*, p. 46.

152: *"Holy habits are"*: Mark Buchanan. *Your God Is Too Safe: Rediscovering the Wonder of a God You Can't Control* (Sisters, OR: Multnomah, 2001), p. 131.

154: *"being still and knowing"*: See Psalm 46:10.

154: *"Cast your cares"*: Psalm 55:22.

155: *"The man who enters"*: John 10:2–4.

156: *"Samuel!"*: 1 Samuel 3:4.

156: *"Here I am"*: 1 Samuel 3:4.

156: *"No, I didn't call"*: See 1 Samuel 3:6.

156: *"Speak, Lord"*: See 1 Samuel 3:9–10.

157: *"ears to hear"*: Mark 4:9.

157: *"The Spirit helps us"*: Romans 8:26.

158: *"And he who searches"*: Romans 8:27.

158: *"If we ask anything"*: 1 John 5:14.

158: *"Teach me your ways"*: Exodus 33:13.

159: *"Enter his gates"*: Psalm 100:4.

159: *"If you remain"*: John 15:7–8.

160: *"living and active"*: Hebrews 4:12.

160: *"My word that goes"*: Isaiah 55:11.

160: *"It's just a spirit thing"*: "Spirit Thing." Peter Furler/Steve Taylor. © 1994 Ariose Music/ASCAP. All rights administered by EMI Christian Music Publishing. Used by permission.

163: *"consider the ravens"*: Luke 12:24.

163: *"consider how the lilies"*: Luke 12:27.

163: *"Go to the ant"*: Proverbs 6:6.

165: *"Give us today"*: Matthew 6:11.

165: *"Where there is no"*: Proverbs 29:18 KJV.

166: *"God's mercies are new"*: See Lamentations 3:22–23 KJV.

167: *"This is the day"*: Psalm 118:24.

167: *"Do not worry"*: Matthew 6:34.

167: *"pray without ceasing"*: 1 Thessalonians 5:17 NKJV.

174: *"The Sabbath was made"*: Mark 2:27–28.

175: *"absolutely a spiritually"*: Qtd. in Tony Carnes, "Bush's Defining Moment," *Christianity Today* 45 (2001): 38.

176: *"Jacob was left alone"*: Genesis 32:24–27.

176: *"Then the man said"*: Genesis 32:28.

177: *"Please tell me"*: Genesis 32:29–31.

178: *"You intended to harm"*: Genesis 50:20.

181: *"By faith Jacob"*: Hebrews 11:21.

183: *"You are the Christ"*: Matthew 16:16.

183: *"I tell you"*: Matthew 16:18.

Part Four

185: *"Until you are surrendered"*: E. Stanley Jones. *Victory through Surrender* (Nashville: Abingdon Press, 1966), p. 65.

189: *"Why you holdin' grudges"*: "Million Pieces." Peter Furler/Steve Taylor. © 2002 Ariose Music/ASCAP. All rights administered by EMI Christian Music Publishing. Used by permission.

193: *"The self is not"*: E. Stanley Jones. *Victory...*, p. 36.

193: *"Seasons are designed"*: Charles R. Swindoll. *Growing Strong in the Seasons of Life* (Portland: Multnomah, 1983), p. 13.

194: *"times of refreshing"*: Acts 3:19.

194: *"fix our eyes"*: Hebrew 12:2.

194: *"a long obedience"*: Eugene H. Petersen. *A Long Obedience in the Same Direction: Discipleship in an Instant Society* (Downers Grove, IL: InterVarsity Press, 2000).

195: *"We are told in 2 Peter"*: See 2 Peter 1:5–8.

195: *"Teach me your way"*: Psalm 86:11.

195: *"The Son of Man"*: Matthew 20:28.

196: *"taste and see"*: Psalm 34:8.

196: *"Search me"*: Psalm 139:23–24.

197: *"Brothers, if someone"*: Galatians 6:1–5, emphasis added.

198: *"If anyone would come"*: Matthew 16:24–25.

198: *"Unless a kernel"*: John 12:24–26.

199: *"Surely you desire"*: Psalm 51:6.

199: *"man after God's own heart"*: See Acts 13:22.

200: *"Therefore, there is now"*: Romans 8:1–2.

201: *"newness of life"*: Romans 6:4 NKJV.

201: *"It is easier"*: Matthew 19:24.

202: *"Who then can"*: Matthew 19:25.

202: *"With man this is impossible"*: Matthew 19:26.

203: *"As unto the Lord"*: Ephesians 5:22 KJV.

203: *"Husbands, love your wives"*: Ephesians 5:25.

206: *"I was hungry"*: Matthew 25:35–40.

208: *"To have a right"*: G. K. Chesterton in *A Short History of England*, Chapter Ten. Quote accessed online at <http://www.cse.dmu.ac.uk/%7Emward/gkc/books/bib.html> (17 June 2002).

209: *"Not seven times"*: Matthew 18:22.

209: *"Therefore the kingdom"*: Matthew 18:23–35.

211: *"twice He cried out"*: See Matthew 26:39, 42.

212: *"If life is water"*: "Joy." Peter Furler/Steve Taylor. © 2000 Dawn Treader Music/SESAC. All rights administered by EMI Christian Music Publishing. Used by permission.

213: *"will fail to receive"*: Luke 18:30. See also verse 29.

213: *"all these things"*: Matthew 6:33.

213: *"complete"*: See John 15:11 and John 16:24.

213: *"the way, the truth"*: John 14:6 NKJV.

213: *"love their life will lose"*: See Matthew 10:39 and Matthew 16:25.

214: *"No soul that seriously"*: C. S. Lewis. *The Great Divorce* ((New York: HarperCollins, 2001), p. 71.

214: *"Let your light"*: Matthew 5:16.

216: *"Just as each"*: Romans 12:4–5.

217: *"We have different"*: Romans 12:6–18.

219: *"If anyone says"*: 1 John 4:20–21.

221: *"city on a hill"*: Matthew 5:14.

221: *"The LORD God"*: Genesis 2:18.

227: *"grow up into him"*: Ephesians 4:15.

227: *"grow in the grace"*: 2 Peter 3:18.

229: *"centurion who came"*: See Matthew 8:5–13.

229: *"He did not do"*: Matthew 13:58.

230: *"became one"*: 1 Samuel 18:1.

231: *"Remember your leaders"*: Hebrews 13:7.

231: *"Where are you?"*: Genesis 3:9.

234: *"Examine yourselves"*: 2 Corinthians 13:5.

236: *"Obey your leaders"*: Hebrews 13:17.

242: *"Be completely humble"*: Ephesians 4:2–4.

243: *"Rejoice with those"*: Romans 12:15.

243: *"If you do"*: Genesis 4:7.

244: *"If you are not"*: Hebrews 12:8.

245: *"No discipline seems pleasant"*: Hebrews 12:11.

245: *"Woe to the world"*: Matthew 18:7 NKJV.

248: *"accuser"*: Revelation 12:10.

250: *"Go and make"*: Matthew 28:19-20.

251: *"Take off the grave"*: John 11:44.

251: *"grow up"*: See Ephesians 4:15 and 1 Peter 2:2.

251: *"Even though you have"*: 1 Corinthians 4:15.

Part Five

253: *"Discipleship means"*: Brennan Manning. *The Signature of Jesus* (Sisters, OR: Multnomah, 1996), p. 91.

257: *"As we lift"*: "It Is You." Peter Furler. © 2002 Ariose Music/ ASCAP. All rights administered by EMI Christian Music Publishing. Used by permission.

261: *"No matter what your"*: Ron Mehl. *Meeting God at a Dead End: Discovering Heaven's Best When Life Closes In* (Sisters, OR: Multnomah, 1996), p. 188.

264: *"We don't always get"*: "Real Good Thing." *Going Public*. Newsboys.

268: *"I tell you the truth"*: Mark 10:29-30.

270: *"My message and my preaching"*: 1 Corinthians 2:4-5.

271: *"We're even more blessed"*: See John 20:29.

279: *"Before we will ever"*: Terry M. Crist. *Learning the Language of Babylon: Changing the World by Engaging the Culture* (Grand Rapids: Chosen Books, Baker Book House, 2001), p. 125.

281: *"Do not let the sun"*: Ephesians 4:26 NKJV.

283: *"harassed and helpless"*: Matthew 9:36.

296: *"I was hungry"*: See Matthew 25:35-36.

297: *"do unto others"*: See Matthew 7:12.

Part Six

299: *"I must keep"*: C. S. Lewis. *Mere Christianity* (New York: HarperCollins, 2001), p. 137.

303: *"Lord, I don't know"*: "Lord (I Don't Know)." Peter Furler/Steve Taylor. © 2002 Ariose Music/ASCAP. All rights administered by EMI Christian Music Publishing.

307: *"If we consider"*: C. S. Lewis. *The Weight of Glory* (New York: HarperCollins, 2001), p. 26.

307: *"Whatever you did"*: Matthew 25:40.

308: *"storing up treasures"*: See Matthew 6:19–21.

308: *"The man who loves"*: John 12:25.

308: *"Why spend money"*: Isaiah 55:2.

308: *"Do not work"*: John 6:27.

308: *"Bread of Life"*: See John 6:35, 48.

309: *"Now this is eternal"*: John 17:3.

309: *"hidden"*: Colossians 3:3.

310: *"I will never leave"*: See Joshua 1:5 and Hebrews 13:5.

310: *"Jesus Christ is the same"*: Hebrews 13:8 NKJV.

311: *"The kingdom of God"*: Luke 17:21.

311: *"Now we see but"*: 1 Corinthians 13:12.

312: *"light and the life"*: See John 1:4.

312: *"for our light"*: 2 Corinthians 4:17–18.

313: *"Turn your eyes"*: "Where You Belong/Turn Your Eyes." Peter Furler/Steve Taylor. © 1992 Ariose Music/ASCAP. All rights administered by EMI Christian Music Publishing. Used by permission.

Song Copyrights

"It Is You"
Peter Furler
© 2002 Ariose Music/ASCAP. All rights administered by EMI
Christian Music Publishing.

"Shine"
Peter Furler/Steve Taylor
© 1994 Ariose Music/ASCAP, Warner Sojourner/SESAC, Soylent/
ICG/SESAC Tunes. All rights administered by EMI Christian Music
Publishing.

"Joy"
Peter Furler/Steve Taylor
© 2000 Dawn Treader Music/SESAC, Soylent Tunes/ICG/SESAC.
All rights administered by EMI Christian Music Publishing.

"Spirit Thing"
Peter Furler/Steve Taylor
© 1994 Ariose Music/ASCAP, Soylent Tunes/ICG/SESAC, Warner
Sojourner/SESAC. All rights administered by EMI Christian Music
Publishing.

"Thrive"
Peter Furler/Steve Taylor
© 2002 Ariose Music/ASCAP, Soylent Tunes/ICG/SESAC. All rights
administered by EMI Christian Music Publishing.

"Cornelius"
Peter Furler/Steve Taylor
© 2002 Ariose Music/ASCAP, Soylent Tunes/ICG/SESAC. All rights
administered by EMI Christian Music Publishing.

"Million Pieces (Kissin' Your Cares Goodbye)"
Peter Furler/Steve Taylor
© 2002 Ariose Music/ASCAP, Soylent Tunes/ICG/SESAC. All rights administered by EMI Christian Music Publishing.

"Lord (I Don't Know)"
Peter Furler/Steve Taylor
© 2002 Ariose Music/ASCAP, Soylent Tunes/ICG/SESAC. All rights administered by EMI Christian Music Publishing.

"Where You Belong"
Peter Furler/Steve Taylor
© 1992 Ariose Music/ASCAP, Soylent Tunes/MS/SESAC. All rights administered by EMI Christian Music Publishing.

These songs can be found on the Newboys' albums:

Thrive

Shine: The Hits

Love Liberty Disco

Step Up to the Microphone

Take Me to Your Leader

Going Public

About the Authors

Peter Furler was born in Adelaide, South Australia. He lives with his wife, Summer, in Franklin, Tennessee.

Jody Davis was born in Petersburg, Indiana. He lives in Nashville, Tennessee, with his wife, Erica, and daughter, Bethany.

Phil Joel was born in Auckland, New Zealand. He lives in Franklin, Tennessee, with his wife, Heather, and daughter, Phynley.

Duncan Phillips was born in Queensland, Australia. He lives in Franklin, Tennessee, with his wife, Breeon, and daughter, Taylor.

Jeff Frankenstein was born in Detroit, Michigan. He lives in Nashville, Tennessee, with his wife, Jenny.

From humble beginnings in church basements and pubs in Australia to sold-out arenas around the world, including Madison Square Garden and the Rock and Roll Hall of Fame, Newsboys have released ten albums. With over 3.5 million records sold, they have 23

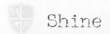

number-one songs, 2 Grammy nominations, and 3 gold records. Their national press coverage includes *USA Today*, "Good Morning America," the *Newsweek* cover feature, *Entertainment Weekly*, and *Teen People*, to name a few. Performing an average of 150 concerts a year, Newsboys are the innovators of the portable touring arena and founders of the annual *Festival Con Dios*.